the
EVERYDAY MILLIONAIRE™
series

The Money Thing Made Easy

Nancy & Brad
I hope this book makes
a difference for you.
[illegible]
6/1/07

the EVERYDAY MILLIONAIRE™ series

Spend smart, dump your debt, and finally put some away!

the Money Thing Made Easy

A *Why-Didn't-I-Know-This-Sooner* Guide for Singles, Couples and Families

HOWARD BONO

Old West Media
EVERETT, WASHINGTON

For information, contact:
Old West Media
1421 Broadway
Everett, WA 98201
coachme@theeverydaymillionaire.com
www.theeverydaymillionaire.com

ISBN 978-0-9793595-4-5

First edition
Book design by Sara Patton
Printed in the United States of America

Publisher's Cataloging-in-Publication
(Provided by Quality Books, Inc.)

Bono, Howard.
The money thing made easy : a why-didn't-I-know-this-sooner guide for singles, couples, and families / Howard Bono. -- 1st ed.
p. cm. -- (The everyday millionaire series)
"Spend smart, dump your debt, and finally put some away!"
ISBN-13: 978-0-9-793595-4-5
ISBN-10: 0-9793595-4-6

1. Finance, Personal. I. Title. II. Series.

HG179.B66 2007 332.024
QBI07-600077

Contents

INTRODUCTION		1
SECTION 1	**Where Do You Want to Go?**	3
Chapter 1	Why People Are in Financial Trouble	7
Chapter 2	The Secrets of the Rich	13
Chapter 3	Your Parents' Money Talk Wouldn't Work for You Anyway	19
Chapter 4	Today's Money Talk	29
Chapter 5	Putting Your Vision into Words	35
SECTION 2	**How Can You Get There?**	39
Chapter 6	New Rules for Your Money	41
Chapter 7	Savers and Spenders	57
Chapter 8	The Ideal Flow of Your Money	71
SECTION 3	**How Are You Doing?**	81
Chapter 9	Keeping Track of Your Money	85
Chapter 10	Dump Your Debt	101
Chapter 11	Your Credit Score	119
CONCLUSION	**Now What Do You Do?**	129

Acknowledgments

Of the many people I should thank for helping me with this book, I am only going to name a few. I'll save the rest for the future books in our series.

To my business coach, mentor, and friend, Rick Ruby—you taught me your system for being accountable and saving money, and my life is better because of your guidance. This book is a result of your teachings.

To my wife, Barb, and my son, Drew—you put up not only with me talking about money all the time, but also with my being gone at night to teach classes. Those classes helped me formulate this information for people who really need it. Thank you for your support.

To the women (the girls) at Old West Mortgage—Patti, Heather, Alex, Jen, and Holly—you took care of things so I could have the time to put this down on paper. Our vision at Old West is to create 1,000 millionaires by helping people understand their money. My hope is that your sacrifice will help us reach that goal of 1,000 millionaires and enrich the lives of all who read this book.

Each player must accept the cards
life deals him or her.
But once they are in hand,
he or she alone must decide
how to play the cards
in order to win the game.

– Voltaire

Introduction

Most people who pick up this book are hoping it will contain the secret to easing their pain.

Readers of books on money usually fall into one of two categories:

1. They already have lots of it and want more.
2. They are having a hard time making ends meet.

The system in this book is for the second group, those people in financial pain—those people who have trouble with the money thing.

I want you to know: If money is a source of uneasiness, discomfort, or actual pain in your life, you are not alone. Millions of American families are suffering with the same issues you are.

Granted, the fact that many others are also struggling probably will not make your journey any easier. Most of us don't take pleasure in others' pain. I simply want you to give yourself a break, and realize that, like most people, you have received no training on how to handle or manage money.

In my mortgage practice, I have evaluated the finances of thousands of individuals and families to reach the conclusions found in this book. I am also a spender myself, and have had to learn how to be responsible with my money.

If you're a spender, too, don't expect me to tell you just to quit spending and save your money to solve all your problems. We both know that will never happen. The funny thing is, born savers don't know it. They think saving money is normal and everyone can do it.

I am a simple guy and I like plain language, so I have made this book plain and simple, too, explaining serious money issues in easy-to-understand ways. You may hear experts say that it is more complicated. My answer to them is, it doesn't have to be complicated unless you really want to have to pay someone to explain it to you.

I have also made this book short, even though getting yourself out of the situation you are in might take some time. But, whether the solutions to your problems come quickly or take awhile, you *can* do it. Just spend an hour or two getting through this book and doing the exercises along the way. And, if you have a spouse, partner, or significant other, get them involved, too. My experience tells me that people who have combined their finances need to be on the same page to make it work.

I'm on your page, too, and, if along the way, you have questions about the systems or how to implement them, just e-mail me at coachme@theeverydaymillionaire.com.

I hope you will now use this book as a vehicle to take you somewhere you've probably never been before, that place where the money thing no longer brings you pain.

Good luck on your journey. Remember, if you stick with it, you *will* make it.

SECTION 1

Where Do You Want to Go?

Putting Together the Money Puzzle

Dealing with money is like putting together a jigsaw puzzle. You have many pieces, each with different characteristics, and they all eventually have to fit together in a certain way.

While you're putting together the puzzle, however, you have some room to try things (all of which might not work) without destroying your puzzle. You can try to put the wrong pieces together, then pull them apart and try again, always looking for the right ones.

When you put together a jigsaw puzzle, what is the most important part? Many people say it's the border, but I believe that comes in second. The most important part is the picture on the lid of the box.

To prove this, play a joke on two of your friends. Buy two puzzles, say, one of a flower and one of a race car. Open the boxes, switch the pieces from one box to the other, and then give them to your friends to put together.

Be sure your friends are good-natured because this will be a very difficult task for them to complete!

The picture on the puzzle box is the map to guide you along

the way, to show you how far you have come and what you still have left to do.

And pictures on puzzle boxes are not just images. They are designed with depth, to help create a feeling when you see them. You can almost hear the sounds in the puzzle scenes, as if they were real. Manufacturers do this on purpose, so you will become totally immersed in the puzzle and its completion.

Working Together

Yes, dealing with your money is also a puzzle. Putting together the many pieces correctly can bring your financial vision to life. You'll end up with all the sights and sounds and emotions you need in order to help take the financial journey you have in mind. And reaching your destination will make your life easier and, almost certainly, much more fulfilling.

One more important word about putting together your financial puzzle: In my work with couples, I have found they are successful only when both are on the same journey and working toward the same vision.

It's not enough for both of you to be working on *a* puzzle. If you're each looking at different pictures on different boxes, it will be impossible to complete the same puzzle. Instead, you have set up a situation in which only one of you can be successful. That means the frustration level usually grows until neither one of you gets what you want.

Now read on for some basic money background, insight into how you got where you are, and rules to help you make a change in direction so you can successfully reach your journey's end.

What does the end of your financial journey look like?

This section closes with a questionnaire to help you to put into words your very own financial vision.

Let's start working on putting together the pieces of *your* puzzle.

CHAPTER 1

Why People Are in Financial Trouble

How Are You Doing?

Most people in America are struggling financially and, sadly, many don't even know it.

To see if you are among them, ask yourself this question:

On a monthly basis, am I . . .

A. Getting a little ahead?
B. Getting a little behind?
C. Staying about the same?

If you answered *A* —

Good for you!

Are you putting money into savings each month?

If you answered *B* or *C*—

- How much more are you spending than you are bringing in?
- How are you covering the difference? Savings, credit cards, loans, trust fund?

When I ask this of my clients, the answer I most often hear is, "We are falling a little behind." Then, however, they have a problem answering the follow-up question. They can't put a number to how much more they are spending than they are bringing in. Where they are financially is more a feeling than actual knowledge.

Your spending habits aren't much different than your weight. Getting a little behind financially each month is a lot like gaining half a pound a month. It doesn't seem like a big deal at the time, but, keep doing it for a few years, and it turns into a really big deal. You'll either have to make some sweeping changes in your habits or just learn to live with the resulting problems.

The tragedy is that many people choose just to learn to live with their financial condition; they give up on the goal of getting ahead. Oh, they still dream of winning the lottery or having a long lost uncle leave them a fortune, but they don't think they can get ahead on their own anymore. In fact, most people won't even be able to quit working without social security or some kind of financial windfall.

If any or all of this describes you, you already know this isn't an awful life. You may be getting along just fine from month to month. You may own a home, have transportation, pay your bills, even have some money in a retirement account. But you probably don't have any money in the bank. You don't have a reserve fund for emergencies or unexpected expenses. When those come up, they get solved with a credit card or borrowed money. Since you already have more debt than you're comfortable with, every time you have to add to that debt for an emergency or unexpected expense, you're just in deeper and deeper. You'd like to change the cycle, but how?

How Did You Get There?

What I have just described is the number one way people get into trouble with their money: *They simply spend more than they have.* A large percentage of our population lives that way, and the group is getting bigger.

Dealing with the money thing when you're in this situation creates a great deal of stress. It's usually not the kind that knocks you down, putting you in the hospital or under a doctor's care. (We don't want to go to the hospital. It's expensive even if you have insurance.)

Instead, it's the kind of stress that always sits in the back of your mind, nagging at you day after day, the kind of stress that creates problems in relationships at home and at work. This kind of stress creates unhealthy lifestyles and, I believe, kills us before our time. I also believe, if we could just get a handle on our money, we could resolve those other issues, too.

I'm not going to let you off the hook too easily by saying that your money stress is not your fault. You, like the rest of us, have made some questionable choices with your dollars and cents. Now, if you were given the chance to do it all over, you'd make some different choices and almost certainly end up with more money and less debt. In other words, hopefully you have learned something from your questionable choices.

Learning What . . . and Where?

Part of the reason you are where you are is that you probably had to learn about money on your own. Very few of us had parents who understood money and were also open enough about it to sit us down and tell us how to deal with it. We got the sex talk instead.

Here's how mine went. When I was fourteen or fifteen, my dad and I were watching the Yankees on TV. My dad loved the Yankees. In one of the breaks between pitches, he said, "Son, do you know about sex?" I said, a little embarrassed, "Of course, Dad. We learned it at school." He said, "Good. Be careful." That was the extent of the sex talk.

As brief as that was, it was still longer than any talk he and I ever had about how I should handle my money.

I have come to realize why parents give the sex talk and not the money talk. All parents have had sex; however, not all parents have had money. They are pretty sure they know how the sex thing works, but they aren't so sure how the money thing works. So, instead of giving you bad advice or bringing up a whole bunch of questions they don't really want to answer, they just don't talk about it at all.

So, most of us get turned loose on the world without any knowledge of how to handle money. We're on our own to make lots of mistakes and pick up what we can from those mistakes. Seems like a harsh way to learn such important lessons.

Rich people, on the other hand, aren't shy about talking with their kids about money. Whether you like rich people or not, you have to admit, being one could be a lot of fun. People with money consider their wealth to be a resource, a tool, something that requires tending and preserving. They view money as a living, breathing entity that must be nurtured.

Tending the Money Garden

My wife has a garden she really enjoys, and here's what I know about it: She makes me till up the soil in the spring, and then she spends an awful lot of time planting, watering, and nurturing that garden.

I can't tell you what all she plants, but I know she's good at it because we eat a lot of fresh berries and vegetables that she grows. We eat corn in the fall and use the stalks for Halloween and Thanksgiving decorations. We always have more tomatoes than we can stand, and, in the winter, we have spicy dill pickles and pickled asparagus. She even plants flowers around the edge, creating a beautiful border to look at while she spends hours doing whatever it is she does in there.

The point of this example is that I don't know anything about plants or gardens. I don't know a daffodil from a dahlia. I could learn if I needed to, but my wife knows how that stuff works, so I don't need to. We have agreed I don't need to be involved at all except for the tilling every spring. And the eating, of course.

Well, when it comes to your money, someone in your family has to know how to tend and preserve it. That person needs to know at least some of the more important things, like how much you make and how much you spend, the difference between an asset and a liability, how to get the right mortgage and an IRA, just to name a few.

Finding Those Who Know

I've heard that, if you want to learn to do something, find someone who is already doing it and copy what they're doing. That should give you the same kind of results they're getting. If you apply this to money, then you should find someone who already has money and has a plan for using it.

This is a hard assignment because most of us won't

walk up to people and ask them if they are rich, how they make their money, and how they manage it. It just wouldn't be polite.

You may not be able to do that, but I can. And I have.

CHAPTER 2

The Secrets of the Rich

The Rich People's Club

People who have money spend time and energy making sure they keep their money. Like my wife tends her garden, they learn how to take care of their money and make it grow. They learn to protect and shelter it. They understand investing, taxes, and the power of giving.

The rich people's club in America is pretty exclusive, but, at the same time, it's one that anyone can join. There's no application, special handshake, or initiation ritual. There are some rules, however. Most people may call them secrets, but they are anything but secret. Here they are, and I've already told you the first one:

The rich spend less than they make, then save and invest the difference.

Most of us will never be able to save enough to become rich, but we do have the ability to *invest* our way there. You start by putting some money away every week or month. No matter how small the amount you start with, it will grow. The key is to start.

When the rich invest, they understand compounding.

This is the prime "secret" of the rich: They understand how compounding creates more money than they could ever earn from their labor.

Let me give you an example. If I told you I'd give you one penny today for your savings and then double your savings every day for the next thirty days, *or* I would give you a one-time payment of $10,000, which would you take?

The cash is a lot of money, and most people choose it and start thinking about what they could spend it on.

But guess how much that penny doubled every day will be worth at the end of the thirtieth day?

$5,368,709.12

Surprised? Rich people aren't. Check out Chart 1 to see how it works.

■ ■ ■

Let's try another one. Take a normal piece of paper and fold it in half. Fold it in half again and then a third time. You've made three folds and now have eight thicknesses of paper. Here is how thick it would be if you folded it over:

- 10 times – the thickness of a ream of paper
- 16 times – the height of a basketball hoop
- 25 times – a little over a mile
- 42 times – to the moon
- 43 times – to the moon and back

If you want to have more money, you must compound the money you already have. Take your extra and learn ways to double and leverage it.

Chart 1: The Power of Compounding

What happens when you double a penny?

Day	Amount	Day	Amount
1	.01	16	$327.68
2	.02	17	$655.36
3	.04	18	$1,310.72
4	.08	19	$2,621.44
5	.16	20	$5,242.88
6	.32	21	$10,485.76
7	.64	22	$20,971.52
8	$1.28	23	$41,943.04
9	$2.56	24	$83,886.08
10	$5.12	25	$167,772.16
11	$10.24	26	$335,544.32
12	$20.48	27	$671,088.64
13	$40.96	28	$1,342,177.28
14	$81.92	29	$2,684,354.56
15	$163.84	30	$5,368,709.12

The rich know the Rule of 72.

This is a mathematical trick to find the number of years it will take to double your investment at a particular interest rate. You divide that rate into 72.

For example, if you are earning 10% interest per year on your investment, it will take 7.2 years to double your money (72 divided by 10).

Or, if you are getting different rates of return each year, just add those rates up. When they total 72, your investment will have doubled.

You can also work it backwards to find the interest rate you'd need in order to double your money in a particular time frame. For example, if you want to double your money in 5 years, you would need to make a 14.4% per year return on your money (72 divided by 5).

By now, you are realizing that investing and compounding your money can help you make great strides toward getting ahead. The Rule of 72 will help you figure out how long it will take.

As shown above, if you make 10% on your investment, you'll double your money every 7.2 years. In our penny example (Chart 1), you need 28 doubling periods to become a millionaire. So, if it takes 7.2 years for each doubling period, you would be a millionaire in . . . just over 200 years. That really doesn't work, does it?

How about if you started with $100? That would take between 14 and 15 doubling periods to make your million—just over 100 years. Still too long.

Starting with $1,000, you'd become a millionaire in 72 years. And with $10,000, you are only 54 years away. But don't get discouraged. The next secret speeds it all up.

The rich leverage their money.

Leveraging allows you to use other people's money to create your wealth. Of course, it can bring more risk, and there are usually some carrying costs, too. But the rewards can be big.

The most common example of leverage is when someone buys a house using a loan for all, or nearly all of the purchase price, and regularly pays just for the interest.

It works like this: You pick out the house you want, in the price range you can afford, and borrow the money to buy it. You may put a little, or even no, money down, and then make monthly payments to cover the carrying costs (interest on the loan).

However, you'll get the increase in value of the whole investment.

I live in the Seattle area, and, over the past forty years, we have seen an average increase in value of 7% per year. Using the Rule of 72, houses in my area double in value every ten years or so.

So, let's say you bought a $75,000 house twenty years ago, and it doubled in value every ten years. That means it has now doubled twice, making your $75,000 house worth $300,000.

If you borrowed 100% of the value of that property when you bought it, and paid only interest (never a penny of the original purchase price), you would still have $225,000 in equity in that property ($300,000 current value minus the $75,000 you still owe on the property). That is leverage—using other people's money to create wealth for yourself.

You can do this in the stock market, equities, property, cars, houses, or just about anything you know a lot about. It's important to invest in what you know so you understand the risks involved. Otherwise you can get yourself into a situation you can't manage. But, if you have to learn about an investment, I believe real estate is the one to take on.

The rich give back.

Whether you call it giving back or tithing or financial karma, it all means the same thing: You can't hoard your money and have it continue to come to you. You have to make sure the money you have is being used to make your life better and just as important, for the betterment of your family and the people around you.

The free flow of money creates more opportunities. This means it has to flow *around* you, not just *to* you. This may sound a little "airy fairy," but all the wealthy people I know give a lot of money away. They understand not only that it is better to give than to receive, but also that you have to give *in order* to receive.

CHAPTER 3

Your Parents' Money Talk Wouldn't Work for You Anyway

The Way Our Parents Did It

I explained earlier that my dad never talked to me about money, but, even if he had, the advice he would have given me probably wouldn't work for me today anyway.

My mom and dad always paid their bills on time, saved money, and owned a home of their own. They did all the things right for their time. They lived and retired comfortably.

If they had given me advice on how to handle my money, here is what they would have told me:

> *Son, here is how you should handle your money.*
>
> *Get a good job with a big company or the government, and that way you will have a good retirement and good benefits. After you get married, save your money for a down payment on a house. Be sure to get a fixed rate mortgage and pay it off as fast as you can. Raise your family and save some money.*
>
> *Then, when you turn sixty-five, you can retire. Since you won't have a house payment, you'll be able to live on your pension and your social security and be comfortable for the rest of your life.*

Sound familiar? Even if you didn't get that advice directly, more than likely it is still the model you are using to handle your money. But this financial model is broken. It is broken because it relies on safety nets that are going away and, in some cases, are already gone.

Back when my dad started out, he knew that if he stayed with the same company until he retired, he would have a pension and guaranteed medical coverage. My parents also had the promise of social security they could collect after they turned sixty-five.

This financial model worked for them because all they had to do was keep working until retirement age, and then all the guaranteed money would kick in.

They knew what they had to do with the money they made along the way in order to be comfortable until retirement. They knew how much they could spend raising a family and still be able to retire, knowing they wouldn't have to earn more money after they retired. They knew when they retired exactly how much money they would get. They had safety nets they could count on.

What Safety Nets?

What are those safety nets, and where do they stand today?

The main benefit my parents had was a *pension*. A pension is a promise your employer or union makes to you, defining the amount of money they will pay you every month after you retire.

The amount you will receive is based on your income and the length of time you put in on the job. Pensions fall under the category of a "defined benefit" plan. This means that the benefit you receive is set, and the company is responsible for making sure there is enough money there to meet the promise. If you don't already have a pension plan set up with your employer, you probably never will, as these plans — more expensive for employers—are going away.

Most companies now offer their employees a *401K* instead of a pension. A 401K is a "defined contribution" plan. That means it is an account into which you get to put part of your earnings, and, in many cases, your employer will match a set portion of your contribution. You don't pay taxes on the money when you put it in or as it grows, only when you take it out. Your employer sets up this type of plan through an investment company. When you put money in, the company adds whatever percentage of your contribution they have agreed to match. With this match, their "promise" has been fulfilled. They don't have to plan for decades in the future.

Within companies' 401K plans, there are usually a handful of levels of risk you can take with your money, and, as expected, the higher the risk, the bigger the possible reward. The way your money is invested within the plan is your choice. You can divide your investments, putting money in one or some or all of the options available. Whatever money you have accumulated (including your employer's contributions) is available to you when you need it. You will choose how and when you receive it.

401K plans are preferred by employers because it is a cheaper way for them to assist you with your retirement. They put money in today and have no future concerns or management responsibility. They don't have to make financial promises they may not be able to keep.

People who have been with companies or unions for long periods of time may still have pensions coming to them. But, if you are not yet receiving yours, keep in mind it is still just a promise and could be subject to change. If the organization can't pay (as United Airlines and Delta Airlines couldn't, to name two of many), they can file for bankruptcy protection from creditors and you then become a creditor. Once in bankruptcy court, lawyers fight it out to decide where your money goes.

I have a client who's been a pilot for a major airline for fourteen years. Because of the problems in the airline industry, his salary has been cut and the pension he has worked for is still up in the air. He's had to re-map his whole financial plan, but he's lucky. He is still young enough to have plenty of time to make whatever changes are required before he needs the money to retire.

I recently read that commercial pilots want to be able to fly until they are sixty-five. Currently, they are forced to retire when they are sixty, but they need the extra five years to save more money because of changes to their pensions and salaries. So much for the promises that companies make.

Would allowing pilots to fly until they are sixty-five make air travel a riskier option? Should companies be forced to keep their pension promises no matter what? Which companies will have problems meeting their promises next? These are all questions we will see debated by the people who make those decisions.

The point I am trying to make is that you have to take a more active part in your own savings plan. Don't rely on someone else to do it for you. You are on your own.

Security?

My parents' other safety net was *social security*. Congress passed this plan in 1935 as a way to guarantee that people would always have something for their retirement even if they couldn't save anything while they were working.

Here is how it works. You pay a 7.65% tax on your wages or salary. (For 2007, it applies only to the first $97,500 you earn.) Your employer matches this with another 7.65%, and all that goes into your account. If you are self-employed, you put in the whole 15.3%.

Of the 15.3% collected from you and/or your employer, 2.9% goes to Medicare and 12.4% into your social security account. Your payments upon retirement or disability will be based on how much money you and your employer have put into your account.

However, here is what the government *actually* does with your investment. All the money goes into the federal government's general fund and, every year, *all* of it gets spent. None of it is saved and invested for you so it will be there when you are ready to retire. In fact, the payments being made today to retired people come from the money taken from your last paycheck.

Based on this method of money management, can the government continue to meet its promises to you? This question is constantly debated but I doubt anyone will really solve it.

As a side note, if a private citizen were to try to operate an investment with other people's money in this manner, it would be a crime. It even has a name. It is called a "Ponzi Scheme."

When you hear about the problems of social security, those

problems exist because all the money is being spent. As the population gets older, this scheme won't work. Fewer people will be working to provide what has been *promised* to those of us who have paid our money.

There is that word—promised—again.

Since fewer people will be paying the bill for more retirees, at some point each worker will have to pay significantly more in payroll taxes. The other option is to change the rules for retirees, who will either receive less money than they expected or wait longer before they can begin collecting anything. The answer will probably be a combination of all those things.

No solution will be easy because it requires the government to admit that it hasn't handled our money correctly and can't keep all the promises it's made. Until politicians find someone to blame it on, they won't even deal with it. They'll just keep patching it up and passing it on to the next batch of lawmakers.

In the meantime, if you want to see what you have accumulated so far, you can contact the Social Security Administration at 1-800-772-1213 to receive a statement of your account. Your statement will show how much has been put into your account and an estimate of your benefits. You can also apply for that statement online. The online application can be found at http://www.socialsecurity.gov/mystatement/. Scroll down and click on "Need to Request a Statement."

The point of what I'm saying here is that the financial safety nets our parents and grandparents were able to count on are either not going to be available to us, or, for a number of reasons, will not come close to providing what we'll need to retire. In short, we are on our own.

Now, it wouldn't be fair to put a scare into you without some directions for how to fix the problems. I am going to show you now the financial plan most families are actually living out *and* what you—and then your children—are going to have to do to make it really work. Please see Chart 2 for a summary of the approaches of all three generations.

Chart 2: Money Rules and Retirement in Different Generations

GREATEST GENERATION (WW I & WW II)	BABY BOOMERS (50s & 60s)	GENERATION X/Y (70s, 80s, & 90s)
Get a job Buy a home Pay it off Raise a family **Turn 60 and Retire** Collect pension Social security Live the good life on savings	Get a job Buy a home Refinance it Get a different job Buy a different home Refinance it Raise a family **Retire?** Collect pension? Spend 401K Social security Survive on savings or keep working	Get a job Save some money Do something for extra money Save or invest it Save more Get different job(s) Buy a home Raise a family Keep home and buy another one Keep that one and buy one more **Retire?** Social security? Spend retirement accounts and savings Live on investments

What the Baby Boomers Have Done

We've talked about how our parents' generation handled its money. Now let's look at what the baby boomers—that generation born in the years from 1947 through the mid-1960s —have done. This is not describing what I recommend you do, but rather, in my experience, what is actually happening.

When boomers get out of school or the military or wherever they've been until they are ready to go out and be adults, they get a job. Once they have that job, they think they have a good thing going so they use credit to buy things they don't want to wait for. They first buy a car on credit; then, when they think they have the world by the tail, they buy a house. When the value of the house goes up—and the debts start to pile up— they refinance the house and pay off the debt.

Most baby boomers change jobs and careers but continue to buy cars and other stuff they can't pay for at the time. Then they sell their houses and buy bigger ones. If there are debts, they may take part of the money made on the house sales and pay them off. They keep the new houses until they go up in value, then refinance them and pay off debts . . . again. Along the way, most boomers raise families and give their kids everything they want.

When they get older and their work life is coming to an end, they end up with some (but not a lot of) equity in their homes, along with some credit card and vehicle debt. There's money in a retirement plan but no money in the bank.

Can Boomers Retire?

The question, then, for many in the baby boom generation is not *when* they will retire, but *if* they will be able to afford to retire at all. Many will have to work until their bodies give out, and then rely on the grace of others to survive. The effort to provide for that generation will be taken up by adult children, charities, and churches, but don't count on the government to take on a lot of it. The government simply won't have the money.

Even if we boomers had used the financial model our parents didn't give us, we still wouldn't be fulfilled since we wouldn't have participated as fully in our consumption-driven generation, enjoying our plentiful years. And we wouldn't be ready for those years to end, either. Even if our houses were paid off and we had little or no debt, we probably would not have the retirement safety nets we need.

The first of the baby boomers will turn sixty-five in 2012 and will want to retire, but many boomers will find that sixty-five is not the magic number for retirement anymore. Not only has the Social Security's retirement age changed for everyone born since 1938, but we also may not be able to afford to retire. We'll have to keep working.

If you have seen the seventy-year-olds working in retail stores and fast-food places, you are experiencing the beginning of a new trend. These people are not there to meet people. They need the money. And many employers are now trying to decide if seventy-year-olds or teenagers are the better employees.

Of course this outline of boomer behavior is not a factual representation of the whole generation. Many baby boomers have saved their money and invested wisely. They have controlled their debts and made good sound choices.

There's no particular type of person who has planned ahead. They range from the disciplined teacher with a nice nest egg, to the corporate executive with multiple homes, to the person creating or building or selling the products and services that fuel our economy. The main thing they have in common is that they all made good choices with their money. Unfortunately, I believe these relative few will be penalized for their good choices in order to make up for the bad choices of the many.

My research shows there are far fewer people living comfortably today than there were in years past. Our day-to-day money is so tight, we are forced to worry about the money part of what happens if our car breaks down or our kids are hospitalized because of an accident. And this doesn't even consider what we'll do when we get older and it is time to live off those children's savings.

Why are we boomers in this situation? Part of the reason is that we have lived most of our lives using a financial model that won't work.

But there is a solution.

CHAPTER 4

Today's Money Talk

What Will Work

Now that we understand our parents' and the baby boomer generations' rules and why they haven't worked, we have to talk about what *will* work. Since I don't have any political agenda or have to apologize for the sins of the past, I'm willing to talk about these failed strategies and about what I believe *you* should do in order to have a good chance at being comfortable with the money thing. This will also give you a shot at living the later years of your life on your own terms.

And these recommendations are also a good place for you to start with your kids. As they get older and the world changes, they will then be prepared to adapt their strategies to those changes and to have a money talk with their kids—a money talk that will actually work.

This model is designed for late baby boomers and for Generations X and Y. The boomers, we know, were born from 1947 through the mid-60s. Gen Xers were born from the mid-60s through the late '70s. Generation Y is made up of those born from the late '70s to the turn of the century. However, for this model, we can lump late boomers with the younger generations because there is still time for all of them to make the strategy work.

The Basics

The first thing you have to understand is:

You are on your own!

- From the moment you start out, every month you have to save some of the money you make.
- When you get a job, recognize that you may not be doing this job forever, so get involved immediately in the 401K plan and save as much as the employer will match.
- Be very careful about running up credit card debt on your future earnings. Just so I make my point about credit cards right away, I believe what has become normal credit card use will—literally—kill you early.
- Most people are going to have some additional way to make a few extra bucks. If you don't, look for one. Even if you make just enough more money to cover the costs of a hobby, it will help. Keep your eyes open for opportunities and try to do something in an area you enjoy.
- Whenever you change jobs, roll all the money that you have in that employer's 401K plan into a self-directed IRA. You only need one self-directed IRA, since you're allowed to roll all 401Ks into it. However, you cannot roll the money from any 401K plan into an IRA until you leave that employer.
- If you live in a market where real estate prices have a history of increasing, do whatever you can to buy

a house. Even if you have to drive an older car and live without an iPod or the latest cell phone, buy a house.

In urban centers, condominiums or co-ops could be a better choice for you but a stick built house is usually preferable. Stay away from mobile homes. There are more and more financing restrictions on them, and that will ultimately affect their value and marketability.

- Your car should not be worth more than 25% of your yearly income. If you make $40,000 a year, you can't afford a $40,000 car or truck. If you are married and make $70,000 per year between you, your cars' values should not exceed $17,500. (This does not include extra cars and motorized toys you own outright.)
- Keep your total debt payments at less than 10% of your gross monthly income. Gross income is the money you make before taxes are taken out. If you gross $3,000 in income per month, your debt payments—on car loans, credit cards, student loans—should not exceed $300 per month. This may sound drastic, but, if you exceed these numbers, you will either be strapped financially or you will never be able to buy a house.
- Once you own a house, stay there for awhile and let it go up in value. Remember the baby boomers in the previous chapter? At this point most boomers would have taken the equity they'd gained in their homes and borrowed it out to pay off debt.

But, if you keep your debt in check, you can do something different with your money, something the wealthy have been doing forever. You can use the equity in your property for leverage into another investment.

The easiest way is to turn your existing home into a rental property and buy another one to live in. But, before you do that, analyze your current loan to make sure it meets your long-term needs. If it doesn't, make a change in your loan before you move.

There are some specific rules to follow in doing this, so contact your mortgage lender or e-mail us at coachme@theeverydaymillionaire.com for a step-by-step description of how to accomplish this. When you have your home financially ready to turn into a rental, then you are ready to buy another property.

I am convinced that this step could be the one thing you do that will provide you with the security we all seek.

However, the growth you will experience on your properties, and the rental income you will receive, will be dependent on your particular market. You have to do your research to make sure that this plan is viable for where you live. And when you're seeking advice on your market, only take advice from people who own rental properties. Others may not understand.

If you are able to repeat this process and buy even one more property, you will have created your own safety net. If you combine this real estate strategy with consistent savings, and with investment in retirement accounts, you'll be able to control your retirement.

What Will Retirement Look Like?

Let's talk about what retirement for each generation looks like.

Our parents and grandparents — that generation that has already retired — have pensions, social security, and perhaps some other retirement options to get them through. Most don't have much debt so they don't have to do much in the way of managing their money. They just get to spend what they receive each month. (This works out well if you are one of those actually receiving enough in your retirement to meet your financial needs. Many are not.)

When the baby boomers retire, they will have combinations of pensions, social security, stocks, annuities, 401K funds, and real estate, and will have to do more to manage their money in retirement than ever before.

This is true because they will have income from so many sources, more debt to manage, and a more complicated tax liability. This combination makes their financial planning the most difficult of any generation in history.

Boomers will either have to figure out how to manage their money themselves, or they will have to pay a professional to do it for them. Instead, unfortunately, many of them will turn this responsibility over to the same kids they never taught about money at all. They probably won't even know what their kids have learned elsewhere because they've already set the family precedent of not talking about it.

Waiting until retirement comes and you need someone to take care of your money, may be a little late to have that money talk with your kids. It's not impossible, but it won't be easy to catch up with what you've been saving your whole life.

If you're in the Gen X/Y group, you will be on your own. You may have some guaranteed income from the sources we've discussed, but you will do well if you make your plans with the idea that those sources will not be available to you. In essence, you will most likely be living in retirement on the money you have saved and the money you have earned through your investments.

Fortunately, if you start now on this plan and spend some time educating yourself, you will be prepared to manage your own money through retirement. And, if you've talked to your kids about money, they'll be prepared to help you.

If you haven't had the money talk yet, you'll probably have to do it on your own. Still, hopefully, you will have set things up well enough that training your kids or hiring a professional can still be done after retirement.

CHAPTER 5

Putting Your Vision into Words

Describing Your Destination

Creating a financial vision is pretty much the same as any other goal-setting exercise — and just as vital. While many people do achieve great things without ever having committed to a goal, I believe that the majority of people who reach the higher levels of success do so by defining their ultimate destination in advance of their departure.

I know that every time my wife and I have ever created a goal, it has happened. I don't pretend to know the power behind setting goals; I just know that setting goals works.

Now, what some people call goals, others call affirmations and others, prayers. Use the term that best expresses your belief, but do take the time and make the effort to set down what you want to have happen in your life.

And make it easy. Just write down what you want to have happen and put a time frame to it. You don't have to put in all the steps. That's way too much work and at this point, it isn't necessary. Just put down *what* and *when*.

Here's a simple model:

My/Our Financial Vision

[This is where you write down what you want. And, if you are a couple or a family, write it that way to help make it more personal and more real.]

My vision is to create a financial life that is focused on taking care of my money. I understand my financial situation and have a plan. I prioritize my spending and live with little or no debt.

I live on less money than I bring in. This creates a more relaxed lifestyle and a more enjoyable life. I set aside two times each month to track my income and expenses and to pay all my bills. I don't bother with my debts except during those two times per month.

[This is where you record how much you want to have at the end of the next three to five years.]

By the year ________ , I have an income of $ ________ per month. I have no debts except for debt on real estate. If I use my credit card, I pay it off every month. I do not have any car payments.

I save _________ % of my after-tax income each month. I have total savings of $ ________________ . The equity in my real estate is $ ___________________ .

[This is where you describe your retirement goals.]

My goal is to create _________________ in savings and real estate equity by the time I reach age _____ . I have _____ years until then.

On Your Way

You have now finished the first section, and, most important, actually written down the beginning of your very own money road map. Keep this map handy because Sections 2 and 3 help add a little more form to your plan.

And congratulations! You are now on your way to your financial destination.

(Even though this book is about money. I encourage you to take a few minutes and write down some things about what you want the rest of your life to look and feel like too. You are on a roll and the extra few minutes could create change in other parts of your life as well. When Barb and I do our goals, in addition to money, we set goals for family, friends, work, spirituality, love life and self.)

6-7-07

5 yr GOAL

* OWN 3 HOUSES: LIVE IN ONE RENT OTHER 2

* RETIRED FROM EMPLOYERS WORK FOR SELF

A * TRAVEL ALOT!!!

SECTION 2

How Can You Get There?

All Systems Go

You are now on the way to your financial destination. But how do you get there?

You use systems.

Systems? That's an intimidating word for something you already have a lot of experience creating and using, probably without even knowing how good you are at it.

Systems provide a structure to do repeatable things the same way every time. In other words, they're simply those little things you do to avoid having to make a new decision every time a familiar situation comes up.

For example, how do you keep from having to look for a towel every time you wash your hands? You put up a hook so there's always a towel handy. That is a system. When you put a cup near the sink for your toothbrush, that is a system. When you put a large can under the kitchen sink for your garbage, that is a system.

These are examples of common systems people use, and they're common because they've been tested and they work. If you put a *large can* near the sink for your toothbrush and a *cup* under your sink for your garbage, you'd have created a couple of systems that wouldn't work easily or for very long.

We want to make sure the systems you have in place for handling your money are easy and workable.

Unfortunately, most people either don't have any money systems at all, or they're trying to use systems that don't work.

Let me give you an example:

> *I will put all my money in my checking account and pay my bills. At the end of the month, I will put whatever is left over into my savings account.*

Have you ever said this and, yet, found yourself without any savings? You created your financial vision and even started a system. The problem is, you didn't create a system that was easily workable for actually making that transfer to savings. Without a complete system, including that final step, it never gets done.

In Section 1, you made a start on creating your financial vision. Good for you! Now, in this section, I'll show you a few very simple systems you can put into place to make it truly easy to handle your money.

Remember: Our goals are to help you make sure your bills get paid on time, eliminate your debt, and put some of your money away. Okay, let's get going.

CHAPTER 6

New Rules for Your Money

The Five New Rules

Systems are the predetermined answers to those questions that come up every day. This chapter lays out the systems you need for day-to-day handling of your money. This is the strategy that people with money use, and you can use it, too.

Here are the five new rules:

1. Get rid of consumer debt.
2. Save some money every month.
3. Invest in your 401K or IRA.
4. Buy real estate.
5. Invest in the stock market.

And here are the systems to help put these rules to work for you.

Rule 1: Get rid of consumer debt.

Consumer debt is what you create when you buy consumer items—cars, stuff for the house, electronics, computers, etc.—with credit cards and on installment plans. While student loans are not consumer debt, they should be treated as if they were. Regardless of the interest rate, you want to eliminate them.

As I mentioned in Chapter 4, payments on your consumer debt need to stay below 10% of your gross monthly income.

But, to move ahead financially, you must learn to live without consumer debt. People who really have money don't have this kind of debt because they pay cash for these items. And when you pay cash, you spend less.

The biggest problem with most people's finances is credit card debt. Now, if you're one of those people getting behind a little each month, you're probably using credit cards to make up the difference. It's a quick solution to the monthly dilemma.

However, I firmly believe that credit cards kill people early. The average adult has more than $9,000 in credit card debt; the average interest rate on credit cards is somewhere around 18%. So, each adult is paying about $135 per month in credit card interest.

How many adults are there in your family? Multiply that number by $135, then add a car payment or two into the mix. Do you see why money is tight every month?

Debt Exercise

- Make four columns on a piece of paper, and use these headings or use Chart 3.

  Name of Debt
  Total Owing
  Monthly Payment
  What Was It For?

  Now fill in the columns. List each credit card and each debt so you can see clearly what you have.

Then total the columns. We'll use this information later on.

Chart 3: Debt Exercise

Name of Debt	Total Owing	Monthly Payment	What Was it For?

Let's talk about ways to clear out this debt. I'm just going to offer some suggestions for you to consider. (And see Chapter 10 for more details on all of them.) Depending upon your situation and your attachment to your "stuff," you may accept or quickly eliminate these suggestions. Keep in mind, however, that it is necessary to completely eliminate *all* the debts in this exercise, if you are to make progress on your journey to the financial destination you've set for yourself.

- *Refinance your house and use the money to pay off all your other debt.*

  This is the quickest way to get rid of consumer debt for people who own a house and have equity in it. And, if you live in a part of the country where real estate prices are going up, you'll simply be using the renewable resource in your home to allow you to start over. I have to caution you: If you do this, you *must* live on less than you bring in and not run up your debts again, or you could put yourself into a situation from which you won't be able to recover next time.

- *Take money out of your savings or retirement accounts to pay off your consumer debt.*

  If you have savings, and can use them to pay off your debts, that is probably a good way to go. If you do have to steal from your savings to get rid of debt, there will be a little pain involved. That's good. Let that pain be a deterrent to running your bills up again.

  I am not a big fan of taking money out of retirement

accounts to pay off credit cards. However, you should not be putting money into a retirement account if you have credit card debt. You should use those retirement contributions to pay off your debt first.

- *Sell your expensive car.*

  As I said in Chapter 4, your car's value should not exceed 25% of your yearly gross income. Whatever your W-2 form says, divide that number by four. The value of your car needs to be below that number.

  The argument that you must be able to afford it or the car dealer wouldn't have arranged the loan for you? Doesn't work. Most people are upside down with their cars. They owe more than they're worth—a loud and clear indicator of the value of the "investment."

  Cars are an expense, *not* an investment. Don't spend more than you can afford. If you are upside down with your car, be sure to add that dollar amount to the chart in the Debt Exercise I hope you have just finished. It's another debt; you have to count it.

- *Create a payment plan using the Debt Eliminator Chart.* (This is Chart 8, found in Chapter 10 and also on our website—www.theeverydaymillionaire.com.)

  This method takes longer than some others, but most people haven't run up their debts quickly. Spending is always easier than saving, so it stands to reason there will be pain in fixing the problem. We'll go into this in more detail in Section 3.

- *Use a consumer counseling service.*

  It's important to note a couple of things about these services. Even though many are nonprofit organizations, they are not free. They do charge a fee and that fee is usually about 15% of the total debt they're managing for you.

  What they do is total up all your debt and then determine your monthly payment. Usually it is a payment on the outer limits of what you can actually afford. You'll make that payment to the counseling service and they will pay your creditors. In many cases, they will negotiate with your creditors to stop future interest from accumulating. But, if the counseling service does not make full payments each month, your creditors will continue to report late payments on your credit report. You could actually end up with worse credit than you started with, even though you're paying your debts.

  One more thing: The fact that you are working with a counseling service will show on your credit report. And many lenders (especially mortgage lenders) look at use of these services in the same way they look at declaring bankruptcy, even though you are paying the debt.

- *File for bankruptcy.*

  This may seem extreme, but it is a legal and valuable method for many people. If you consider this, contact an attorney in your state and ask lots of questions. Rules for how this is handled vary depending on both the amount of your debt and

> the amount of your income. In some cases, you're allowed to keep your house and car, and even your retirement account.
>
> A bankruptcy attorney will be able to give you more accurate advice based on your financial situation. Be aware that attorneys charge by the hour and can bill more hours if you do file bankruptcy, but can't bill hours to you if you don't.
>
> After you file for bankruptcy, you'll have a difficult time obtaining new credit for a few years. You will still be able to buy real estate, but there will be more limits on how much you can borrow and on the rates you will pay.

I hope one of the above options will work for you. If you have questions about your particular situation, e-mail the details to us at coachme@theeverydaymillionaire.com, and we'll respond with some suggestions.

Rule 2: Save some money every month.

This is absolutely critical to having a satisfactory financial plan. Most people have money tied up in their houses and in retirement accounts but nothing in savings. This means that when things come up—and they do—they have to borrow money to fix them.

You must have a ready savings account. Ideally, that account should be equal to three months' worth of living expenses, but, for now, let's just concentrate on putting *something* away every month.

If you are contributing to your company's 401K plan, you

are already saving every month, but you don't see the money and don't have easy access to it, so it stays there. We need to learn how to do that with the money we do see, from our regular paychecks.

How? Know how much you are spending each month, and designate some money for savings when you are paying your bills. If one of your "bills" is a check to your savings account, it will get paid. But, if you wait until the end of the month and just put whatever is left into your savings account, it will not get done. And the proof? It hasn't happened yet, has it?

(Don't worry—we'll get to specifics on how you handle this in Chapters 8 and 9.)

Rule 3: Invest in your 401K or IRA.

First, never forget: If you have credit card debt, you need to pay that off first before putting money into any retirement account.

I repeat: *Do not put any money into a retirement account until you pay off your credit card debt.*

Now, as you know (see Chapter 3), a 401K plan is a retirement account your employer sets up for you to put money in directly, right out of your paychecks, before you pay taxes on it.

Many employers agree to provide some kind of matching funds. That will be up to each individual employer; they are not required to match anything.

If your employer does promise, for example, they will match fifty cents on every dollar you contribute up to 8% of your income . . . well, this is free money. By all means, take it.

But contribute to your 401K only the exact amount your employer will match. Not a penny more. If your employer will not match any of your contribution, do not invest in your employer's 401K plan. There are better options for your money.

You see, 401K plans may not be as great as they appear on the surface. I know—here's another thing that goes against what you thought was right. So, let me explain.

Congress passed legislation in 1978 changing the tax code to allow these plans, which are based on three simple ideas:

1. People could earn more money on their investments if they could put it in and let it grow without paying taxes on it.
2. Employers could help out their employees without having to provide pensions.
3. When people took their money out after retirement, they would pay less in taxes because their income (smaller than when they were working) would put them in a lower tax bracket.

Let's see if this is really such a good deal.

If you were a farmer and I was the government, and I gave you the choice of paying taxes on the value of the seed that you plant or the value of your harvest, which would you choose? The seed, of course. Your crops will be sold for much more than you paid for the seed, right?

Retirement plans like the 401K and traditional IRA make you pay tax on the harvest. Will you or Uncle Sam be better off in the future with that plan? You've seen what compounding your money can do (Chapter 2). Would you rather pay taxes on your money before or after it's compounded?

Let's also analyze the argument that you will be in a lower tax bracket when you retire.

First, when you retire, do you want to be in a lower tax bracket? Is that what you're striving for? Is that the financial vision you created in Section 1—to have *less* when you retire? No, of course not.

We are all striving to have a big pile of money from which we'll be drawing income after we stop working. Using the Rules of the Rich (Chapter 1), especially compounding, it is possible you could have more income in retirement than you had when you were employed.

Now answer this question: Do you think the percentage of taxation that the government will be charging you ten or twenty or thirty years from now, will be a lower number, the same number, or a higher number than it is today?

Based on past experience, don't you think it is probably going to be a higher number?

Okay, so if you are going to pay a higher rate of tax and you are striving to have more money in your later years, is a 401K or traditional IRA the best place to put your money? I don't think so. So, that's why my advice to you is to put in whatever money your employer will match—and not a penny more.

Fortunately, there is another option. You can open a Roth IRA which allows you to pay taxes on the money you put in. Then your investment will grow tax-free, and you can take it out tax-free, subject to federal guidelines.

In my opinion, a Roth IRA is a better investment for you. And the government must believe it, too, because they limit the amount you can invest. The 2007 limit is $4,000 per person age 49 and younger. If you are 50 or older you can invest up to $5,000 per person. This applies unless you have a taxable income of about $150,000 or more. (An accountant or tax professional can give you the specifics.) When you get to this level, you cannot contribute to an IRA at all. You can continue to contribute to a 401K, however.

You can open an IRA at your bank or credit union. Your insurance agent sells them, too, and so do stockbrokers and financial planners.

When you open a traditional IRA or a Roth IRA, you'll be able to invest those savings in anything available on Wall Street — stocks, mutual funds, money markets, commodities, bonds, and even real estate. Everything is open to you, which may make your choices more difficult. Be sure whoever sets up your IRA explains your options to you.

Rule 4: Buy real estate.

If you want to create wealth, you have to own real estate.

All of the wealthy people I know at the very least own the houses they live in. Almost all of them have more than one property, owning either a second (or third) home or rental properties, or both.

If you ask real estate owners if they've made money on it, they will say yes. If you ask how they actually did it, they'll tell you the value of the property went up after they bought it. They may have made some money by paying down the principal, but the bulk of the money they made as owners came from price appreciation. These equity gains can be really high, especially in areas where real estate is going up in value quickly.

Don't believe for a second that you already missed the real estate window. You haven't missed it anymore than the people who didn't buy in the '70s missed it. There's plenty of future appreciation left to make millions of people wealthy. In other words, there is still a lot of money to be made in real estate.

I coach my clients to buy real estate and plan to hold it for the long haul. This way they experience the compounding effect on a highly leveraged investment.

If you have made money on your house, as most people have, would it have been a good investment to buy the one next door, too? If you had done that when you bought yours, and your neighbor had been paying you rent, what would your financial position be today? If you ask wealthy people, many would say this is exactly how they made their money.

Of course people have concerns about housing prices and about dealing with renters. When you invest your money, you have to invest in your knowledge, too. To be a homeowner, you may not need to know much. But, to be an investor, you have to learn a few things.

Recently, we have been bombarded with talk of a housing bubble. First, I want to say that housing prices are different around the country, and the way housing prices move is a regional characteristic, not a national one. There is no such thing as a *national* housing bubble.

The reason housing prices change is very simple. They move based on the law of supply and demand. The details, of course, are more complicated, and there are hundreds of factors that are used to predict and monitor housing price movement.

But, in short, if you live in an area that people are moving into and where jobs are available, that's a good sign. If you have to act quickly to buy or rent a house because other people are trying to buy or rent the same house, you are probably in a market seeing rapidly rising housing prices. There's enough demand in that area for housing that it puts pressure on the supply.

If, however, you are in a market or town with a higher unemployment rate, you may be seeing more people leaving than moving in. If it takes months to sell a house, and buyers are making offers well below what sellers are asking, you are in a market where housing prices are stagnant or even dropping. There is more supply than is necessary, and the lack of demand is creating downward pressure that makes it hard to sustain current prices.

A local real estate agent can be a good resource for information on your particular market. Make sure you talk to one who has experience and also owns at least one or two properties. Look, too, for someone who is in the market with their own money. A real estate license does not automatically mean the information you will get is accurate or practical.

Rule 5: Invest in the stock market.

If you have a 401K or an IRA, you are already in the stock market, and, before you do anything more, be sure you are already living by the first four rules above.

The stock market, like ownership of rental properties, requires some education. The problem with getting educated about the stock market is that it can be expensive. In order to talk to a stockbroker with some experience, you have to have some money to invest. The more money you have, the more experienced the broker you'll get to work with.

If you have $10,000 ready to invest, you are probably going to work with a rookie straight out of college. They may be more energetic and willing to answer your questions, but they are using your money to learn how to be brokers. If you are going to work with one of these beginners, you need to do your homework in advance so you can follow what they are doing with your money.

I prefer working with a broker who has learned with someone else's money. I want to trust my money to someone with experience in the ups and downs of the market. But, to work with an experienced broker, you'll have to have at least $100,000 to invest. Some require $500,000 or even $1,000,000 to become one of their clients.

These are big time guys and they play for keeps. Go into a local stock brokerage company. You'll see nice offices, lavishly furnished. Their business is geared to the bigger players. If you have enough money, they will teach you what you need to know.

My broker, Kurt, is an old friend who I think was born to be a stockbroker. He's been in the business, and with the same firm, for many years. He handles my money the way he handles his own, and I stay out of it. I monitor the statements each month but I don't need to take the time to learn the ins and outs of what Kurt has spent thirty years mastering.

I guess you could say my relationship with my broker and my stock investments is like my relationship with my wife and her garden. I know what my job is, so I do it, and then enjoy the benefits of their knowledge and work.

I do believe you need to have money in the stock market to really gather wealth, but it usually requires a detailed and time-consuming education to be successful. You may want to start out by looking into money market and mutual funds. They're available from brokers and banks, and many insurance agents sell them, too. When evaluating these funds, past performance is usually a good measuring stick for gauging future profits. Always be sure to get the advice of an expert before investing your money.

Having said all that, if you pay attention to the news, you've seen some high-level executives go to prison for manipulating stock prices. This is a high-stakes game, and it is usually the smaller players who lose their money and don't get it back. Be safe; don't be greedy.

■ ■ ■

There you have them, the five new rules for handling your money, and some beginning systems to help make them work for you. Follow these rules, and you'll be much farther along on your financial journey. But don't stop here. The fun part is still to come!

CHAPTER 7

Savers and Spenders

Opposites Attract

This is my favorite discussion within the whole subject of money and budgeting. I've never read anything else about this most critical topic, and I don't know why. After all, unless you understand the dynamics between savers and spenders in your life and your relationships, you're missing the key to making any kind of money agreement work. Without that understanding, you may make agreements; they just won't be agreements you can keep.

They say that opposites attract, and I find that a lot when working with couples. The most common dynamic at work in the couples I've helped is that one is a spender and one is a saver. As we delve into how this plays out in spending, saving, and bill-paying habits, you will understand what you need to do to fix your own particular situation.

Advice from One Who Knows

Before we go any further, I want to come clean: I am a terrible spender. That means I really understand the spender's mindset.

Now, it first seemed odd to me that I, a spender, would be helping others understand how to manage their money. Then

I thought, who better to help people understand money than someone who has had to learn the hard way to handle his own? I also have experience with the "opposites attract" thing in my family, as my wife is a saver.

In other words, you are getting advice from one who knows.

Characteristics of Savers

Savers aren't just savers; they are non-spenders. That means they're not looking to buy things like spenders are. They actually avoid it.

I believe savers, by nature, have a deep down feeling that they are never going to have enough. They prioritize where their money needs to go, and their first priority is always to put it away for a rainy day. I'm from Seattle and we have lots of rainy days. So, if you're a saver, I'll bet this is resonating with you and you're preparing for rainy days, too. Savers put money away in case of . . . everything!

Most savers, however, never get to the point where they believe they are prepared enough. I have a friend with more than a million dollars in the bank who doesn't feel like she could weather the storm. Conversely, we hang out with a couple with no money stashed away at all, and they are always the life of the party. (Yes, they are both spenders.)

If you're a saver, you must identify how much you need to save every month and how much you need in the bank in order to feel comfortable. When you start negotiations with your spender-spouse, come armed with this information so you can get what you need, too.

Exercise for Savers

Analyze the following questions and write down your answers:

- How much do I need in the bank to be comfortable that I have enough?
- Is it a dollar amount?
- Is it a percentage of my monthly spending?
- Is it just making sure that I am spending less than I bring in each month so that my savings continue to grow?

Characteristics of Spenders

Spenders are always looking to "make the buy." We are adrenaline junkies who get some kind of rush from acquiring stuff. There's a need to fill, and spending money fills it.

Spenders all have different needs and different degrees of "spendiness" (my word). But none will respond the way you want them to, when you tell them just to stop spending. It isn't going to happen. It's like telling a smoker just to quit smoking. If smokers do quit smoking, it's because they made that decision on their own, not because they've been told.

Most of the reformed spenders I know now have money in the bank and enjoy guilt-free spending. I'll show you later how to organize *your* guilt-free spending money.

Exercise for Spenders

Analyze the following questions and write down your answers:

- How do I like to spend my money?
- Cash, credit card, debit card, checks, other financing?
- How much do I have to spend at any given time to meet my need to spend?
- How often do I have to do it?

Let me give you some examples of how completing this exercise can help spenders get a better hold on the money thing.

I have a client, Sara, who is a single mom and also a spender. When Sara answered the questions above, we found she needs to spend $50 at a time and use cash. If she does that once a week, she doesn't do anything stupid with the rest of her money just to meet her need to spend.

The solution we came up with was to have Sara buy her groceries once a week instead of making one big trip per month. Now she stops on the way home from work before she picks up her kids. Her short grocery trip feels like a little spending spree just for her. Sara has met her need to spend for the week, and did it responsibly with money she was spending anyway. Now she has more money because she is not wasting money just to buy something.

I have another client, Bob, who had to buy big things. Bob

bought a motorcycle and, less than a year later, a boat. Like most spenders, he didn't have the money, so he financed them. Bob is married, but was able to buy and finance both purchases without his wife even knowing, much less agreeing. Sadly, he is still out of control, but, now that they've filed for bankruptcy, he can't get credit for those big purchases any longer.

What kind of solution is available for Bob? He would be a good candidate to become a buyer for any kind of company that deals with big-ticket items. He would really love his job, getting to spend money all day, and he might be able to fulfill his need to spend without destroying his personal finances.

Which One Are You?

Before we really begin to explore the dynamics of spender-saver couples, it's important to determine which one you are. Don't try to straddle the fence here; you will have a dominant side. Just go with it. You are one or the other.

Here's a little test. It is the tenth of the month. The early-in-the-month paycheck is gone, and the middle-of-the-month paycheck won't be here until next week. You have unpaid bills and there isn't much food left in the fridge. Now, if you find a $50 bill, will you pay bills or go out to dinner? Your answer will tell you if you are a saver or a spender.

Now that you know for sure which you are, let's talk about the family dynamics of savers and spenders.

You'll have noticed that I'm gearing this discussion to couples. There's a reason for that. If you are single and a saver, you already have a good handle on the money thing. If you are a single spender, you can still get by just fine by following the rules and setting up the systems. In fact, when we get into the actual nuts and bolts of all that, you'll find it makes spending money fun again.

The Saver-Saver Household

Let's talk first about a household made up of two savers. They will have the easiest time accumulating wealth. Savers are typically not party animals; in fact, you might even think they are boring. But, before you pick on them too much, you need to bear in mind that they are probably pretty comfortable and have money in the bank.

If you go to dinner with a saver-saver couple, they will either duck out when the bill comes or want to break up the check so they pay exactly what they owe. Nothing more. If we remember their belief that they will never have enough, we can understand why they behave this way. If you're a spender, you may be inclined to pick up the tab. The savers will let you do it; they will be grateful, but they *will* let you pay.

Savers are usually organized people. If you go into their homes, you will find some kind of system for keeping track of things. They'll probably have a pretty complete method for handling money and paying their bills. You'll find a comfortable house but it's not filled with lots of knickknacks. Savers don't shop the QVC Channel because they don't want to spend their money on stuff. They won't have the latest big screen TV, and, if they do have a big item or an expensive car, they did mounds of research before they concluded it was a good investment and bought it.

In other words, if your household includes two savers, you are probably not reading this book.

The Spender-Spender Household

The dynamics change when you have two spenders. They have credit card debt—lots of credit card debt. They're fun to go out with because they know how to have a good time, and, when the bill comes, they are grabbing for it. (If the waiter comes back and whispers something to them, they will have a backup credit card that will accept this purchase.)

A two spenders' home is full of cool stuff. They have plasma TVs, fun electronics, and great cars. They have nice furniture and many neat things to make their house a little more showy.

Spenders have minimal organizational skills, but, somehow, they manage to get the bills paid. Neither of them wants to pay the bills, so one of them takes on the job but hates it.

Most important, two spenders have lots and lots of debt and no savings. They have no savings because, when spenders look in the checking account and see $500, they start thinking about things they can buy with that $500. This is just the way we are wired. We are not looking to save money; we are looking at what can we buy to get that spending rush.

And, when you have two spenders together, they feed off each other and talk each other into buying even more things.

The Saver-Spender Household

What happens when you have both a spender and a saver in a family? When the saver controls the money, they probably have good credit. Remember, savers are usually organized and will make sure the bills get paid. The saver also understands that, if they don't pay their bills and end up with bad credit, they will be charged more for interest. If they are charged more for interest, there will be less money available in case of

. . . . Are you starting to feel what the savers are feeling?

This family probably does have some money issues. After all, the saver controls the money and doles it out to the spender, and savers don't have any idea what a spender needs. You can't stop spenders. They will find a way to keep spending, say, opening a credit card, or two or three, that the saver doesn't know about. Spenders will hide money. I've even seen them take on extra side work and jobs, without the saver knowing. Then they can spend without the saver knowing, too.

This family will have credit card debt, probably more debt than the one trying to manage the money knows about. Of course, they usually will have some minimal savings because the saver has stashed away money the spender doesn't know about.

Their house does have some extras because the saver occasionally gives in and lets the spender buy things. But this couple doesn't have a financial vision and doesn't want to have any discussions about money. Why not? If they try to have an air clearing discussion about their money, one of them may have to lie. It's just easier not to talk about it.

The Spender-Saver Household

But what about the family with both a spender and a saver, in which the spender controls the money? Most of the time that I see this combination, the wife is the saver and the husband is the spender, but the husband (spender) controls the money for some reason. Of course, the wife can be the spender in this scenario, but, in my experience, that's not the common structure.

This family has hidden debt because the spender has created more debt than the saver knows about. Besides, just as with the saver-spender household, they can't talk about money because one or both would have to lie.

They do have some minimal savings. Why? Because the saver has put money away that the spender doesn't know about. That is the only way this couple will save any money. They have average-to-poor credit because the spender — with more debt than the saver knows about — has to shuffle things around when paying the bills in order to keep it hidden.

Their house is comfortable, but with lots of items that look out of place. They've got older furniture but a huge TV, or really nice cars with hand-me-down everything else. The spender buys things without any kind of strategy. See it. Buy it. The saver tries to organize what the spender is doing but is fighting a losing battle.

Can These Relationships Last?

What do you think about the longevity of these spender-saver relationships? Are they more or less likely to make it than couples that are both savers or both spenders?

I believe they are less likely to make it because there's this big, important part of their life they can't talk about. They have secrets, and they don't work together. In a sense, they are always sabotaging each other's efforts.

Remember the idea that dealing with the money thing is like putting together a jigsaw puzzle (Section 1)? Mixed saver-spender couples often don't even know whether they are putting together flowers or race cars.

I've already told you that I'm a spender and my wife is a saver. Well, she controls the money in the family and it's working. But, at first, she had a hard time understanding she was not going to change me. She was going to have to work with me.

I repeat: Savers, you are not going to stop your spenders from spending; it is not going to happen. Your spenders are going to spend.

So let me show you how to harness it.

The Solution

If you're a saver, you have to handle the money. You are better equipped to put some away because you don't have to spend it just because it's there.

If you're a spender, you really don't want to take care of the bills anyway. Spenders handle the bills only to have access to the money.

Hey, spenders! What if you had access to money and didn't have to do all the bills? Wouldn't that be perfect?

With some honest discussions and lots of negotiation, my wife and I came up with a solution that works perfectly. We've been using this method for years, and never argue about money. She does question some of the stuff I bring home, but, as long as I keep my agreements, I can buy anything I want.

In other words, our money discussions are now productive, and we are moving forward toward our financial vision. What has made the difference? We agreed that the only possible solution was to get me out of the family budget. We tried many things but here is what finally worked:

- I get an allowance every two weeks. Over the years, I have negotiated increases in my allowance, and it is a very comfortable one.

- My allowance goes into my own separate account at a different bank from the one where we keep our family account.
- My wife does not know how much is in my account. Our agreement is that it is none of her business. She has a spending account, too, and the balance in hers is none of my business.
- I follow these simple rules:
  - I can buy anything I want.
  - I don't have to pay any bills out of my account.
  - I can't use *any* credit.
  - I can't touch the family account.

Spenders, how are you liking this so far? This is the guilt-free spending account I told you about earlier.

Savers, can you see the benefits of getting your spender out of the household account? When your spender comes home with some new thing you are sure you don't want or need, you can still be excited for them because you know it didn't affect the family budget.

Two Spenders: Is There Hope?

Before we go further into the specific systems that make this saver-spender solution work, I want to address the family with two spenders. Here is the only way I have seen this combination work:

- Both spenders must have their own separate spending accounts.
- Neither can carry a credit card. (Spenders, you know what happens when you have a credit card.)

- When you handle the family money and pay bills, you must do it together. That way, you can keep each other honest. It is not that you're dishonest people, but money often leads you to make bad decisions.
- Set aside an hour or so to do this, twice a month. And make it fun. Do it after dinner, with a bottle of wine and the kids at the grandparents . . . whatever you have to do to make it enjoyable. That way you won't skip over it. This is important, and could save you in the future.

Setting Up the Systems

Open separate bank accounts, preferably at separate banks. If you do choose to keep them at the same bank, make sure the statements come in separate envelopes. You must stay out of the other person's account. This just won't work unless you can each have your own money.

Next, determine how much money goes into the spender's account every pay period. This has to be an honest talk, with family budget limitations in mind.

I promise you, if the saver simply dictates to the spender the amount of money he or she will get, the problem will not be solved. Savers can usually live on less than spenders. Spenders must be allowed to have what they need.

Savers, take note: Spenders who *honestly* agree to an amount will hold up their end of the agreement. If an amount is forced upon them, even though they may agree, it is a shaky deal at best. Until the spender really agrees, keep talking and keep working to find the right number.

In Section 1, we talked about needing to find additional ways to make money. In many cases, this is how people come to an agreement about spending accounts. Spenders agree to take a guaranteed allowance that is less than they really want, but they get the extra money they make on the side. That way there is additional incentive to make more money.

Let's say the spender has the option of working overtime. If they work overtime or do a side job, they may agree to give half their additional income to the house account, and then they get to put the rest in their spending account. Of course, all this is negotiable, but opening up the discussion will allow you to create your own rules, agreements, and systems—rules, agreements, and systems you don't have now.

If you are still hiding money issues, you must deal with them. In my mortgage practice, I sit down with clients and we go through each of these items. Many times it is as much marriage counseling as money counseling, but, if you are willing to do this, you can make it.

If you are trying to work this out and have questions, e-mail us at coachme@theeverydaymillionaire.com.

CHAPTER 8

The Ideal Flow of Your Money

The Ideal System

Most people don't have any kind of system for how to handle their money, and I didn't either. Then, a few years ago, my business coach told me, if I changed the way I handled my money, I would have more money to handle. Since he had more money than I did, and because I was paying him to coach me, I did what he recommended. My wife and I started to use his strategy, and it worked.

Based on our experience using it, we've made some modifications to his original plan and have come up with what I call *The Ideal Flow of Your Money*. Refer to Chart 4 to see what it looks like.

And read on to find out how it works, and, most importantly, exactly how you can make it work for you.

Banking Basics

To start with, you will need these bank accounts:

- A joint checking account

  (Couples: This is an account you both sign on. Most come with a savings account, too, which you also need.)

Chart 4: The Ideal Flow of Your Money

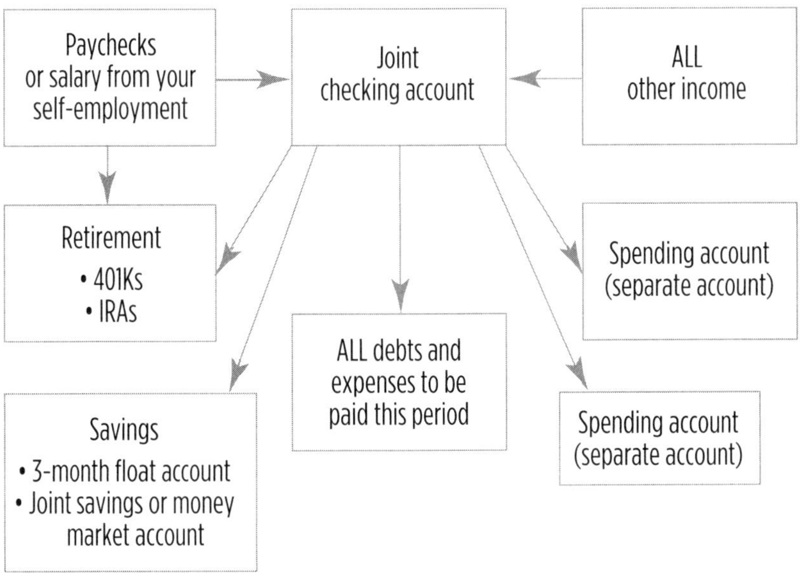

- Separate checking accounts

  (Each person will need his or her own separate checking account for a spending account. The savings part of this account is optional and will be used only if the person whose account it is, chooses to use it.)

Your salary and wages can get into your checking account in a variety of ways, but many people now use direct deposit because it is easier for employers.

This is a critical mistake, especially if your money is already tight, and this mistake can be compounded if there is a spender in the family. Why? It is too easy to start spending money before you even know how much will be in the account.

I encourage you to stop your direct deposits and, instead, arrange to receive paper checks that you have to take to the bank yourself. Even if you only do this for a few months while you get up to speed on this system, I am confident you will see the difference—and have more money.

Once your bank accounts are set up, start taking care of your family's money like businesses take care of theirs.

For example, *all* your money needs to go into your joint checking account. You cannot take cash out of your checks, pocketing it before the check goes in. If you do, there is no way to keep track of it. The only exception is contributions to your 401K. The law requires that 401K contributions be taken directly out of your paycheck.

Every business has a checking account into which all its money goes initially. However, businesses don't store their money in a checking account long term, and neither should you. Your money only stays there long enough to determine how much is there. Then it's distributed.

How to Pay Your Bills

Determine a place to put all your money-related mail. Some people put it in a binder; some use a file cabinet. In our house, we have a kitchen drawer for bills.

When a bill comes in, my wife opens and reviews it to make sure it's accurate. She keeps the return envelope and payment stub, then throws the rest away. (That way, when she is writing checks, she's not wasting time dealing with all the extra paper.) The bill goes in the drawer and is ready for her next scheduled money distribution day.

Ideally, you should pay your bills once a month. That requires less overall time, and, if you structure it correctly, you still won't have any late payments. (Keep in mind that late payments don't show up on your credit report unless you are a full thirty days late.) On most debts, you can call the creditor and request your due date be changed, in order to make it easier to pay bills all at the same time.

Once you get started on the once-a-month system, you'll never want to go back to dealing with it more often.

Despite the advantages, however, some people either can't, or don't want to, do this job just once a month. So, if the once-a-month schedule doesn't work for you, pay your bills twice a month. Set up two specific days each month for taking care of your money.

Many people can't stand to have unpaid bills in the house, so they use the twice-a-month system to move them out more quickly. But don't try to pay your bills once a week; that requires too much time. You'll find yourself spending more time sending your money to other people and less time enjoying your money yourself and with your family.

Again, set aside one or two times per month to do this. No more.

Income and Outgo

When you sit down to pay bills, begin with two stacks of paper.

One stack is your money to deposit — paychecks, rental checks, any other income. By having your checks right there, you'll know you haven't pre-spent any of the money you've planned to use to pay the bills you've scheduled to pay at this time.

The second stack is of the bills that need to be paid.

The first thing to do is actually pay the bills. As you write each check, enter the amount in a single-sheet budget form. (A copy and an explanation of the form will be found in Chapter 9.)

Once you have written all the checks necessary to pay your bills, you then write the checks to put money into your spending account(s). Whatever money is now left goes into your joint savings account. (Remember: You will need to retain some amount in your checking account to keep it open. Each bank has its own rules on this.)

You won't use your joint checking account again until the next time you pay bills. All the spending until the next money distribution day will come out of your spending account(s).

Congratulations! What you have just done is handle your money like wealthy people do! They take care of their commitments and savings first, then spend the rest.

In Between

You're now probably wondering how you pay for gas and groceries and other things you spend money on between paychecks. Of the dozens of ways to handle this, let's talk about a few.

When it comes to filling up your vehicles, each person could have gas money added to their spending account for that period. For example, if you spend $50 per week on gas, and you refill your spending account every two weeks, then add $100 to the amount you can spend, and continue to pay cash for your gas.

Another way is to get a gas card, put all your gas purchases on that card, and then pay the card off every month with the rest of your bills. This is a good option because you'll know exactly what you spend on gas, and the spender will also have less cash available to spend possibly in a wrong area. If you use this method, don't put any other purchases, like food, on that card. Keep it for gas only, so you can easily track what you actually spend on gas.

Yet another option is to keep cash on hand at the house just for gas. However, this may again be too tempting for a spender, and absolutely should not be used in a family with two spenders. If you are a spender, and your need to spend is satisfied by cash, you should always use a gas card, because, if you are carrying enough cash to pay for gas, too, you will probably spend it elsewhere before you get to the pump.

Food is another item you'll usually need to buy between pay periods. In most families, grocery shopping is handled by the same person each time. If that's the case, take the grocery money and put it in the spending account of the grocery buyer.

I have also known people to get cash and put it into envelopes labeled for groceries and gas. Some people even use envelopes to cover spending for their kids.

Any of these systems can work as long as you come to an agreement on the system and, then, give the system time to work. Check your exercises for spenders and savers (Chapter 7) to make sure you're making agreements you both can keep. Having too much cash around the house could prove to be too tempting.

Putting Some Away

The most important thing is not to spend money out of your joint checking account all month long. Unless you follow that rule, you'll have no extra money to work its way into your savings account.

Once you put money in your savings account and get used to having it there, you will become possessive of it. You'll find yourself keeping it instead of spending it on things you really don't need and haven't researched.

Here is a good rule for buying medium-to-large items: Never buy on impulse.

Instead, when you decide what you want, wait two weeks before you actually make the purchase. If, after two weeks, you still want it, buy it. It will then be a well-thought-out purchase you will enjoy even more.

However, you'll soon find that many of those purchases won't be made, and the money will stay in your savings account. Now, this doesn't work if the clothes dryer dies, and you have to buy another one. But it does work when considering new rims for the old car, or even choosing between the 42" and 65" flat screen TVs.

Your goal is to accumulate in savings an amount equal to three months of your regular spending. If all your money stopped coming in, how much would you need each month to maintain the same lifestyle? We call that number your monthly survival number.

Of course, until you keep track of your money for awhile, you can't know what your survival number is. That's the reason for our budget form (Chapter 9).

How Would You Feel?

My goal for you is to have no debt except on your real estate, comfortable spending and saving habits, and three months of your survival number in the bank. Take a moment to think about how this would feel. Wouldn't you sleep well at night?

With this plan, you *will* get there. Many of our clients already have. And you will find that, as you start to make more progress on your financial journey, your money worries will start to dissolve.

The beauty of this plan from a spender's perspective is that you take a little time each month being responsible with your money, and the rest of the time can focus on spending without guilt. As you develop the system, and your debts decrease, you'll also find that you have more money for spending. It just gets to be more fun.

From a saver's point of view, this system includes constant building of a savings account to provide security. Since savers are looking for security, this monthly accumulation will make the saver in the family much more comfortable.

Next Stage of the Journey

You have now just about finished Section 2. But, before you move even closer to your financial destination, it's time to look again at your Vision Statement from the end of Section 1. You'll need to make a few additions based on your new knowledge.

Updating My/Our Financial Vision

Remember the new rules for your money as you revise your financial vision. They are:

1. Get rid of consumer debt.
2. Save some money every month.
3. Invest in your 401K or IRA.
4. Buy real estate.
5. Invest in the stock market.

You must also understand how the spender-saver dynamic works in your situation.

- Who is/are the saver(s)?
- Who is/are the spender(s)?
- Who will handle the money?

Include the results of the exercises for spenders and savers in your vision.

Then answer these questions:

- For the next six months, can we agree to handle our finances based on the Ideal Flow of *Our* Money?
- When will we open the new bank accounts necessary to accomplish this?
- When will we change our direct deposit paycheck(s) to paper check(s)?
- When will we have a discussion to determine how much will go into our separate spending accounts?
- Can we agree to wait two weeks before making any medium-to-large purchases?

This will only take a few minutes to put down on paper. And, even if only one of you writes it all down, it is vital that the other person participates.

Remember: If you're a saver and your partner is a spender, you will have to do all this. You'll have to get them to read the vision and agree to it. They won't want to be too involved, but it isn't because they don't care. It's because their mind just doesn't work that way. To make this work, you just have to give your spender enough money to keep them out of your way.

But, if you put in the time, this does work—for both of you—and reaching your financial destination will be within your grasp.

SECTION 3

How Are You Doing?

Copying the Best

The highest-paid people in our society are those held most accountable for their results. Do you know who they are?

Athletes
Entertainers

I'm sure you'd agree that these people live in a different financial world than we do. They also follow different rules. In terms of their accountability, athletes and entertainers have three things in common:

1. *They keep score.*

   With athletes, it's obvious. But entertainers are serious about keeping score, too. As soon as a TV show is over, executives know how many households were watching and what percentage of the viewing audience they got. By Sunday night, producers know how much money their new movie brought in over the weekend. Whether consumers buy a CD or download a song, record companies know exactly how much money is brought in. The results are broadcast to the world on the top-seller charts. People in the entertainment business are very serious about keeping score.

2. *They practice more than anyone else.*

   Again, with athletes, this is obvious. However, entertainers rehearse over and over again before they show what they've been working on. The purpose of practicing is to make sure you know in advance what you're going to do before a situation comes up. You've heard the phrase, "Practice makes perfect." That's not quite accurate. Rather, "Perfect practice makes perfect." And, believe me, they practice, practice, practice.

3. *They all have coaches.*

   On the field or in practice, athletes have people to help guide them, to watch and advise them, so they can be sure they are doing everything they should in order to achieve the best possible outcome. Entertainers have these people, too. They're called directors, voice coaches, hairstylists . . . and the list goes on and on.

If the highest-paid people in the world are held accountable for their results, why wouldn't we do whatever we could to copy them? After all, the best way to accomplish a task is to find those who are already doing it well, and do it the same way.

Now, I'm not suggesting you give up everything and become an athlete or entertainer. What I *am* suggesting is that you copy some of the behaviors of these people who already have money.

In this final section, I will show you how to find out how well you're doing with your money—how to keep score. You already know I'm a spender, so my advice won't be just to stop spending. Yes, it is possible to spend money and still remain accountable to your future success. Let's get into the nuts and bolts of how to do it.

CHAPTER 9

Keeping Track of Your Money

Controlling Your Future

This is the step that stops most people from really understanding their money. However, when you don't understand where your money goes, you are giving up control of your future.

Does the word "budget" stir up in you negative emotions in the same way words like "diet," "taxes," "homework," and "dentists" do? People get tied up in the emotion of budgeting before they even get started. But, if you've read this far and done the exercises, you are almost to your financial destination. Don't stop now!

You already know that the rules, agreements, and systems I've presented will decrease the amount of time it takes you to deal with your money. You already know that I still want you to spend money. In fact, not only won't you have to stop spending, but you will no longer have any guilt about spending. You already know that people with money handle their money this same way.

So open up, and give this simple system a try. I promise you that it's really pretty easy and relatively painless—and will have a big payoff in your future.

When you start this plan, do it the old-fashioned way. Write everything down on a piece of paper, then add it all up. For the first few months, actually writing down the figures will help things stick better in your brain. After years of doing it manually, my wife and I are just now starting to put it on our computer to "automate" it. You may make that transition to the computer more quickly, but I still recommend that you start by writing it down.

In the last chapter, we discussed the actual mechanisms for writing checks and setting up the accounts those checks are coming from and going into. Now, in this chapter, we'll deal with the art of keeping track of all that. The only additional work required is transferring the numbers you already have, onto your budget form.

Why is this so important? It reduces your monthly "*money thing*" to one piece of paper. I don't know how to make it any simpler than that.

Step By Step

I'm now going to take you through that one-page form, step by step. You can use a copier to enlarge Chart 5 to its full size, or download it from www.theeverydaymillionaire.com.

To make this as easy as possible to follow, I have numbered the different columns and spaces you'll be filling in so I can explain them one at a time. (Chart 6 includes those numbers.)

Here we go . . .

Chart 5: Family Budget Form

Month: Year:

Name and Balance of Debt	Minimum Payment	Amount Paid	Income
TOTALS	**Survival Number**	**Checks Written**	**Total Income**
Necessary Float Balance (Survival Number x 3)			

Amount Saved
This Month
Year to Date
Float Account Balance

401K Balance
401K Balance
Other Savings
Equity in Home
Equity in Rentals
TOTAL ASSETS

Chart 6: The Budget Form Explained

Month: Year:

Name and Balance of Debt	Minimum Payment	Amount Paid	Income
#1	#2	#3	#4
TOTALS	#5 **Survival Number**	#6 **Checks Written**	#7 **Total Income**
Necessary Float Balance (Survival Number x 3)	#8		

Amount Saved	
This Month	#9
Year to Date	#10
Float Account Balance	#11

401K Balance	#12
401K Balance	#13
Other Savings	#14
Equity in Home	#15
Equity in Rentals	#16
TOTAL ASSETS	#17

1. Name and Balance of Debt

In this column, you will list each bill.

Start with your house payment or rent, followed by payments on other houses, then on cars, credit cards, and any other consumer loans and lines of credit.

To establish some common language, I will use the term *consumer debt* to mean money owed on car payments, credit cards, installment loans, and lines of credit not attached to your house. More generally, consumer debt is any debt that is not a mortgage. So, you should also include doctor bills if you are making monthly payments directly to your doctor, and, if you have any unpaid collection accounts, list them in this column, too. Unless you have already made a payment arrangement, just note the debt and the total amount owed.

When you list your consumer debt in Column 1, start with your car(s). Next list the rest of your consumer debt (credit cards, installment and student loans, etc.), starting with the one with the lowest balance and then the rest in order from smallest to largest. Also include the total balance owed for each debt. This number will change every month and is listed on your monthly payment statement.

Next, move on to your utilities. Include heat, water, power, phone, cable, internet, and any other utility-related debts. Since you pay these in full each month, you do not need to list total debt in this column. Just write the name of the debt.

Now list your automobile expenses, too. Insurance and gas are the most common, but you may have others.

Be sure also to include groceries, dining out, and other household spending money. Of course, if you have kids, there will always be a range of expenses from doctors to daycare. Be sure to list them all.

At the bottom of the column, keep spaces for your 401K contributions and for your savings and spending accounts. You can combine whatever you choose to make things fit, but you must make sure you can keep track of all your money on this page.

This letter-sized form should be large enough to cover your budget unless you own lots of properties or you have too much consumer debt. If you need a larger sheet, a legal-sized version is available for downloading on our website.

One of my goals for you is to eliminate all your consumer debt, but add enough properties that you will need to use the legal-sized form.

2. Minimum Payment

In this column, list the minimum amounts you must pay to meet your agreements for this month.

This is your *actual* house or rent payment. When it comes to credit cards, be sure to list the *minimum payment* due for that month. If you have a gas card, the entire amount is your minimum payment. Gas cards have to be paid in full each month. If you can't do that, get rid of the gas card.

You may have other bills that are due every two months or car insurance that you pay every six months. To plan ahead, use the average monthly balance of those less-frequent bills in the minimum payment due column.

This is an important column, so be as accurate as you can. Your first month or two, you will have to do some estimating and, probably, flat-out guessing. This is a great way to start.

It will be fun to go back in future months to see how close you were.

3. Amount Paid

After you've written your checks, put the amount you *actually* paid for each item in this column.

If you are paying a little more or a little less than the minimum payment (on a credit card, for example), your entries in Columns #2 and #3 will be a little different. If you are paying a power bill that comes only every other month, record here the actual amount of your check for *this* month.

4. Income

Now for income. In this column, list separately each check you'll be depositing and its amount.

For paychecks, list the amount *after* the deductions for taxes are taken out. If you are having 401K contributions taken directly out of your checks, make a separate entry and include that amount in this income column, too. Also record your cash from tips or side jobs.

You have to understand where every bit of your money is coming from, and the actual amount you are getting. If you are guessing about these things, it means you're not using all of your money well. You have to keep track, especially in the beginning.

Now, you may have made an agreement that some or all of your "extra" cash (from side jobs, etc.) will go straight into your spending account. You may not want your saver-spouse to know exactly how much money you have. But do keep track of it at least until you have eliminated all your consumer debt. Once you don't have any debt, your spending account will get increased anyway, so this shouldn't be an issue.

5. Survival Number

This is the total of all the minimum payments required to meet your needs for the month — your survival number (Chapter 8). This will change each month, but, after a few months, you'll be able to see a pattern and establish a pretty tight range for what your survival number really is.

6. Checks Written

This is the total of all the checks you've written for the month, and it *must* equal the total in #7. This way you are keeping track of all the money you brought in and all that went out. (Don't worry — this isn't as strict as it sounds. Remember that your spending account allows you to spend that money without keeping track or being specifically accountable for it.)

If #6 is smaller than #7, congratulations! Put more money in savings to balance them out. If #6 is larger than #7, you will have to take money out of your float account to make them match. Until you have enough savings, most people will use credit cards to balance the sheet. In either case, record it honestly so we know what to fix.

7. Total Income

This is the total of all the money you actually brought in for the month. Again, #6 and #7 must match.

Now, take a look at #5 and #7. If the total in #5—your survival number—is larger than the total in #7, you are spending more than you are bringing in. In Chapter 1, we talked about the fact that most people are in that boat and don't really know it. There will be more tips later on fixing this problem.

If your total in #7 is larger than #5, the difference between them is the extra money you have available this month for working on saving and investing, using the laws of compounding and leverage. This is your seed money for making your move to getting ahead on your financial journey.

8. Necessary Float Balance

Take your survival number (#5), multiply it by three, and put that number in this box. This is the goal for your float account. Some people call it a rainy day fund, but I like to call it a float account because it goes up and down.

Once you start to build it up, you will become very protective of your float account. This number will change slightly each month because your survival number will change; however, over time, you will find that the necessary balance for this account won't vary too much.

9. Amount Saved This Month

Show here how much you have saved this month. Be sure to add in what you put in your savings account(s), your 401K contributions, and any other money you have somehow put away. The initial goal for this box, your monthly savings, is 10% of #7 (your total monthly income).

10. Amount Saved Year to Date

This is the running total of the money you've saved so far this calendar year.

It's a figure that the average person, couple, and family has absolutely no idea about. If they wonder about it at all, it's a passing thought because there is no system in place to make this number available. But all the people with money do keep track of this. That way they know from month to month how they are doing.

My wife and I use this number to make our New Year's resolution for the upcoming year. It is simple, we can easily keep track, and we can reassess the number up or down during the course of the year.

11. Float Account Balance

This is the total of how much you have in your float account.

Most people use the savings account tied to their checking account to keep this money. Others put this savings into another bank so it's harder to get at. As your account grows, it probably makes more sense to put it into a money market account, which will pay you a higher interest rate and still provide quick access to your money when you need it.

12 & 13. 401K Balance

These boxes contain the balances in your 401K and/or IRA accounts.

You want to list these separately from your other savings accounts because they are not readily accessible, and you don't want to tap into them unless you absolutely must.

14. Other Savings

This also could be labeled stocks or money market or any number of things. This is where you record all your savings that are not in a retirement account or your float account. As you add more of these types of accounts (for example, accounts with different brokerage companies, mutual funds, college or insurance accounts), you may choose to add separate boxes on this form for them. That will be up to you. Initially, however, start with this one box, and build from there.

15. Equity in Home

If you own a home, you need to know this number.

Take the value of your house and subtract what you owe on it. (Keep in mind that a line of credit on your house is a mortgage, too, so also include that debt.) The difference between your home's value and what you owe on it is your equity. Put that number here.

You may be wondering how you can determine the value of your home. There are websites that will give you a number, but I won't list them here because I don't believe many of them are very accurate, unless you live in a well established "cookie cutter" neighborhood.

Instead, it's a good idea to connect with a local real estate agent who will do a free "Comparative Market Analysis" (CMA) on your property. Real estate agents work on a commission, so be fair; let them know you aren't going to sell your home now. A smart agent will understand you could be a great client in the future and will gladly prepare the report for you. If you find agents who are not willing to do this, move on. They're not worthy of your future business.

Actually, it's helpful to have a relationship with a good real estate agent in your area even if you are not buying or selling right now. They can keep you informed about the market, and, when you are ready to buy another home or investment property, you have already established trust with a person who can help you.

16. Equity in Rentals

This is the equity in your investment property or properties. Determine their value and subtract what you owe, just as you did for your own home for #15.

17. Total Assets

Here is the total of all your assets—your savings and the equity in all your property. Add the figures in #11 through #16 for this number.

To calculate your net worth, take the total in #17 and subtract your consumer debt (listed in #1). Your net worth is the amount of money you would have left over if you sold everything and paid off all your debts.

Net Worth Exercise

To see what your financial life would be like if you had to live just on the money you have already saved, take your net worth and multiply it by .0046. This is the amount of the monthly check you would receive.

This is based on putting all your net worth in an investment at 8% interest per year, and taking out only the interest after taxes.

Taking a Stab at It

Right now, sit down and fill out Chart 5 from memory (a blank budget form is on page 98). Try to list your debts, approximate balances, and monthly payments. Estimate your food expenses and other spending money. (Chart 7 shows you what a completed form looks like.)

If you are like most people, on your first try, you won't even be close.

Couples, each of you should fill out one on your own, then share your results when done. This will shed some light on where you are today, and clearly show if the puzzles you are building are even similar.

Savers, you may have to tie up your spenders to get them to do it, and they probably won't want to participate again, but make them do it anyway. It will be one of the most valuable things you have ever done.

Then, once you get the first month's budget form completed with actual numbers, share it with the spender so they have an idea of the whole picture. Then send them off with their spending account, and they'll be happy and out of your way.

But don't worry. Even with your spender gone, you are not alone. If you have questions about this form, e-mail us at coachme@theeverydaymillionaire.com and we'll get your questions answered.

Happy spending.

Family Budget Form

Month: Year:

Name and Balance of Debt	Minimum Payment	Amount Paid	Income
TOTALS	Survival Number	Checks Written	Total Income
Necessary Float Balance (Survival Number x 3)			

Amount Saved	
This Month	
Year to Date	
Float Account Balance	

401K Balance	
401K Balance	
Other Savings	
Equity in Home	
Equity in Rentals	
TOTAL ASSETS	

Chart 7: Sample Budget

Month: January Year: 20XX

Name and Balance of Debt	Minimum Payment	Amount Paid	Income
House payment $173,500.00	$1,255.00	$1,255.00	
Car – Ford 18,975.00	422.00	422.00	
Car – Honda 8,451.00	261.00	261.00	
			Paychecks
Sears 322.00	10.00	10.00	$1,427.55
Bon 988.00	30.00	30.00	1,427.55
Visa 4,375.00	110.00	110.00	973.95
MasterCard 10,546.00	210.00	210.00	973.95
Food	600.00	600.00	Other income – like tax refunds, rents, or unexpected money – goes in this column
Power	152.00	152.00	
Natural gas	85.00	85.00	
Phone	84.00	84.00	
Cable	65.00	65.00	
Water, sewer, garbage	70.00	70.00	
Cell phone	50.00	50.00	
Insurance	150.00	150.00	
Spending	400.00	400.00	
Savings		549.00	
401K		300.00	
TOTALS	$3,954.00 **Survival Number**	$4,803.00 **Checks Written**	$4,803.00 **Total Income**
Necessary Float Balance (Survival Number x 3)	$11,862.00		

Amount Saved	
This Month	$849.00
Year to Date	$849.00
Float Account Balance	$2,644.00

401K Balance	$8,455.00
401K Balance	6,545.00
Other Savings	
Equity in Home	52,000.00
Equity in Rentals	
TOTAL ASSETS	$69,644.00

CHAPTER 10

Dump Your Debt

Imagine . . .

Remember the New Rules for Your Money (Chapter 6)? Why is the first rule—the number one priority—to get rid of consumer debt? Because consumer debt is what stands between most people and their having extra money each month.

Imagine how much money you would have left over each month if you had no consumer debt. No car payments, no credit cards, no student loans.

Imagine a life in which you have no consumer debt but do have three months' worth of your living expenses in the bank. How would you sleep at night? How would you handle those little things that are an annoyance because they cost money? I'll bet you would handle them differently than you do now.

I want you to have the opportunity to experience that feeling.

You must be completely focused on this goal of getting out of debt until it has been achieved. That means you not only have to accomplish the task of dumping your debt, but you also have to learn to live on less than you make so you don't run your debt back up again.

For the record, I ran my credit cards up twice, five years apart, before I learned. Most of us aren't born with this understanding; we must be taught. My experience with credit cards taught me that the most lasting lessons are often the hardest to learn.

Dump It Where?

When I talk about dumping your debt, I don't mean you just walk away from it and let someone else pick up the pieces. Filing for bankruptcy is the only legal way I know for doing this. No, when I talk about dumping your debt, I mean dumping the burden you are bearing with that consumer debt, and feeling instead the relief that will be yours when it is off your shoulders.

There are lots of scams out there trying to convince you that you can eliminate your consumer debt, and even mortgages, without paying them off. I've helped people clean up the financial devastation these plans have left, but I've never seen one that actually worked. They really exist to separate you from even more of your money.

You can't really get ahead using these schemes. Instead, you'll find yourself watching over your shoulder. Someone will always be looking for you, and you'll just have more of a mess to clean up later.

Here's the alternative. I encourage you not to focus on how to get out of your debt, but how to make good on it. If you take shortcuts to accumulate wealth, there will always be someone to take it away from you when you get there.

Cards That Can Kill

You've heard me say this before, but it bears repeating: I truly believe consumer debt will kill you.

Consumer debt is helpful to our economy as a whole. Consumer debt keeps people buying things, which helps businesses expand, which creates more things for people to buy.

Don't get me wrong. I love consumerism. I'm a spender. I feel in my soul that buying things is great. Toys are great. It's just using consumer debt to buy this stuff that doesn't work, debt actually takes all the fun out of it, and, yes, I believe it can shorten your life.

How? It's the stress of all those sleepless nights, and of having to deal with annoyances that turn into emergencies because you have debt instead of savings.

Consider just your credit cards. In Chapter 6, we talked about the credit card debt that families are carrying today. If you have $18,000 in credit card debt at 18% interest, you are paying $270 per month in interest alone.

Think about that. You could pay $270 every month forever, and you would still owe $18,000.

Now the credit card companies are trying to make sure you don't get too bogged down in interest. With some prompting from the federal government, they have raised the minimum monthly payments on their cards. Instead of amounts from 1½ to 2% of the outstanding balance, they now require minimum monthly payments of 3 to 4% of the outstanding balance.

That means, in some cases, your minimum payment could be more than double what you were paying. Now you will pay off your cards more quickly, but most people won't be able to afford the monthly sticker shock.

So, if your card now has a minimum 3% monthly payment, you'll be forking over $540 a month on your $18,000 debt.

The good news is that you'll pay your debt off completely in only four years while paying "just" $7,380 in interest.

Or, if your card now has a minimum payment of 4%, you'll have to come up with $720 per month. At that rate, you'll retire the debt in less than three years while paying a little more than $5,000 in interest.

Sounds better, but there's a problem. Payments that size, especially when combined with other debt and expenses, are just too big for most people to keep making for years at a time.

Fine Print

Have you ever read the back of a credit card agreement? You had to sign that agreement to get the card. Did you read it? Don't feel bad; almost nobody has. Here now, in plain English, is how it actually affects you:

> *We, the credit card lender, can do anything we want to you, at any time, for any reason. In fact, we can create new rules at any time.*
>
> *We can also raise your rate. Yes, we can lower your rate, too, but we won't unless you threaten to take your $10,000 debt somewhere else. Then we will lower it to keep you, and raise it again as soon as we can.*
>
> *We can use every trick available to get you to spend more so you will owe us more. If you don't pay, we will hound you and wreck your credit for years to come. And, if we have to use lawyers to get the money we encouraged you to spend, you'll pay all those costs, too.*

Now, this is an oversimplification and satirical, but it's still not too far off. In 2005, banks and credit card companies pushed through a change in bankruptcy law that made it more difficult for people to file for bankruptcy to eliminate credit card debt.

By the way, they then decided to help you pay this debt off more quickly by increasing your minimum payments right after the new bankruptcy laws went into effect.

The bottom line is, credit companies are ruthless when it comes to getting you to spend your money and well-funded when it comes to getting you to pay it back. Quit doing business with them.

The Card You Need

So, let's review.

The average family pays more than $500 a month on credit card debt payments. Those payments can change at any time and you will just have to keep paying.

Statistics also show that, when you use a credit card, each purchase is an average of 22% more than if you paid cash. Why? Because in the heat of the purchase, it feels like free money. We know it isn't free though, don't we?

You will pay and pay and pay until you finally quit using them. But—and here's the kicker—even then, you *have* to have one. In our society, without a credit card, it's nearly impossible to make airline reservations, rent a car, or buy online.

With the credit card odds stacked against you, what do you do?

You really do need to have one, so get *one*—one with a $3,000 maximum limit. Use that card only when you must, and pay it off in full, before the due date, every month.

Of course, when the credit card companies see that you are handling your money responsibly, they'll use the trick of raising your limit. They'll call it a benefit, a reward for your good behavior, but it really is just a trick to get you to spend more. Tell them to leave it at $3,000 or you will cancel the card and deal with someone who will abide by your wishes.

This is how you can use the credit card companies and their money. Even though many of them have already found ways (and are looking for more) to charge you for using their money in this manner, it's a small price to pay compared to what you have been paying.

Dump It How?

By now, you should have a single piece of paper showing you the total of all your consumer debt and the monthly payments necessary to stay current with that debt. (Chapter 6 included the Debt Exercise, and Chapter 9, the budget form showing your debt.) To reach our financial destinations, we need to live on less than we bring in each month, and the biggest hurdle to that goal is usually consumer debt.

So let's focus on some specific systems you can use to lower your consumer debt. Read the possible alternatives described below, and then decide which one is the most comfortable for you.

Finding the Money

The fastest way to make consumer debt go away is to take money out of your bank account and pay it all off. If you can't do that, borrowing the money at a lower interest rate with lower payments is the next best way.

But banks hate to lend money without collateral. They like having the legal right to something of yours that has value, something they can come and get if you don't pay them. For most people, that means their car or their house.

I deal in mortgages, and, in my opinion, using your home equity to clear up consumer debt makes the most sense for the largest group of people. You can usually borrow up to 100% of the value of your house at a lower interest rate than you're paying on your current debt. You can also stretch the payments out over a longer period of time, which will lower your overall monthly expenses.

This reduction in payments may allow you to start living on less than you bring in so you can start putting some money away, if you haven't been doing so already. Your payments may be tax-deductible, too, but I don't recommend making decisions solely on tax implications. When you have lots of money, taxes will become more of a factor. Let's get you there before we worry about that part.

As I mentioned earlier, cashing out your home equity to pay off consumer debt is a new way of thinking, and my ideas are not without their critics. Here are two comments critics make—and why I think they're wrong:

1. *If you borrow the money out of your house, you end up paying off your credit cards for thirty years.*

   This is 2007, not 1957. You are not going to keep your house that long, and you are certainly not going to pay it off evenly over the next thirty years.

   Let's say you use $20,000 . . . $30,000 . . . $50,000 . . . or even $80,000 of the equity in your home to pay off your consumer debt. Over time, your home will increase in value and you will have paid off your debt with money you did not have to work for or pay taxes on. It will feel like you paid off the debt for free. We know that isn't true, but it will feel that way.

The length of time this will take depends on the value of your house, and on the economy and future growth of real estate in your part of the country. Look back at the price of houses in your area five, ten, or twenty years ago. Did your house increase much in value? Is that growth likely to continue? I believe it is.

2. *You can't count on your house going up in value. It is not a stable investment like the stock market.*

   I think this is a ridiculous argument. Remember what the famous Will Rogers said:

   "Buy land. They ain't makin' any more of the stuff."

   If you could go back in time and invest in anything you wanted, what would you buy? If you had specific knowledge of the timing of the stock market, you might buy stocks and do well. But you could randomly buy land anywhere, and, today, it would be worth many times what it was worth then.

   If that is true, why can't you use real estate as a vehicle to wealth? The short answer for most people is that you can, and, in fact, real estate is the best way to reach that goal.

Real Value in Real Estate

I believe if there were a way to present a real estate report on the news each night as there is a stock market report, more people would understand this important steppingstone to wealth. If we had cable channels dedicated to real estate and real estate investment, we would better understand the benefits of using ownership of property as the basis for our investments. If becoming a real estate professional was as difficult and as lucrative as becoming a stockbroker, real estate *would* be the basis for investment.

But the big money in our society is largely tied up in the stock market. Stock can be created out of thin air at any time. Its value can be manipulated, and its paper wealth can be inflated or destroyed in an instant. Real estate is slower, harder to get your money out of quickly, and does not make it easy to artificially manipulate the price.

If you own a house, here's an easy question: Have you made more money on your house or in the stock market? If you don't own a house, is your next goal to buy one, or to own more stocks?

Using your house to right your financial ship is a valid way to organize your finances. You just need to make sure you are in the right situation and you have a plan for how to move forward.

The worst thing you could do is to use your equity to clear out your debt and then run your debt up again. Using the equity in your home to eliminate your consumer debt *must* be a one-time shot to get you back on your feet. You can't keep doing this and expect to end your working days with anything but a bunch of stuff and no real money. And you will need real money, not stuff, when you stop working.

"Retiring" Your Debt

I have a client who uses his retirement accounts like bank accounts. If you have money in an IRA or a 401K, you could take it out and pay off your debt.

If you do opt for this way of dumping your consumer debt, just take the money out and use it. Do not borrow it and then pay it back. Just take it out.

And, remember, if you do take it out, you will pay a 10% penalty, and the amount you withdraw will be taxed as normal income in the year you take it out.

If you choose to do this, the person you talk to from your 401K plan will probably try to talk you into borrowing the money and paying it back to yourself with interest instead of taking it out and paying the penalty and taxes. Don't do it. That won't help your monthly expenses much, and you will still be paying consumer debt. That won't help you learn to control your own money and get used to living without any debt. You are just trading one debt for another, and still paying it back with money you have to earn from your job. That is not how investors do it.

Now, despite all that, I am not a fan of taking money out of retirement accounts to pay consumer debt. However, if you don't own a house, this may be your best option. If it is, do it and don't look back. You will be able to increase your retirement income many times over if you are not harnessed with that debt.

As I have said more than once before, if you do have consumer debt, you should not be putting new money into a retirement account until you get rid of that debt. Always use those retirement contributions to pay off your debt first.

Make It Count

If you don't have a house or a retirement account to draw from, you're going to have to find another traditional way to pay off your debt—look to relatives and friends for help. Maybe you can get a loan, or even a gift, to clear things out. The goal is to eliminate your debt as fast as you can with the least amount of monthly expense.

Again, if you have not organized your finances so this won't be repeated, you are not ready to take this step. Make sure you have a solid plan in place so you will be living on less than you bring in. You know, if you go to relatives or friends to bail you out, they may do it, but they will only do it once. Make it count.

If you can show them this will be a one-time need, they will be more likely to help you. And, if you're successful, the friend or relative who helped you will get a real sense of fulfillment, too. Make sure to keep them informed of your progress.

The Hard Way

If none of the previous recommendations work, you will have to do it the hard way. You will have to change your spending habits and create a payment plan to pay off each debt one at a time.

Start with eliminating the debts you can. The most noticeable will probably be the expensive car with a big payment. If you have one, and it's at all possible, get rid of it. If you can't get rid of it, refinance and get the payments down. That way you can take the extra money and get rid of the other bills faster.

If you do start driving a cheaper car, this will bring your

debt situation into public view. Your friends and family will wonder why you're driving a car that is not as nice as the one you had. You can make up a story or you can tell the truth; it's up to you.

If you tell the truth, however, you will open the door for others to tell you their stories of how they're in the same situation you are. I have seen the finances of thousands of people. Most people you know need some help with their money. This book might be a good gift for them.

The next thing you will need to do is create a schedule to show how you are going to pay off your debt. We have created a form called The Debt Eliminator (Chart 8) to help you organize the payments. Like the other charts in this book, it can also be downloaded from www.theeverydaymillionaire.com.

Though this method takes a longer period of time to pay off all your debts, you will see results right away.

Start by determining the minimum monthly payments for all your debts, and then figuring out how much extra you can add to that number each month

Let's say you have been making $850 in minimum payments per month on your debts, and you are now going to take my advice to put your 401K contributions on hold until you've eliminated those debts. Since you've been contributing $400 a month to your 401K, you'll now be able to pay off debt at a rate of $1,250 per month. Let's see how we make that larger amount go even farther.

List your debts on The Debt Eliminator the same way you did on your budget form, from smallest to largest. If you have collection accounts, these get listed, too. Then start at the bottom of the list, making the minimum monthly payments on

Chart 8: The Debt Eliminator

How much extra are you going to pay each month to reduce your debt? $ ________________________

Name of Debt	Minimum Payment	Balance Owed	Amount Paid This Month	Months Left to Pay Off

each item. When you reach the smallest debt, apply everything you have left of your $1,250 to that item. Most people will actually be able to pay off a debt or two completely in the first month. This is a quick win and these debts are gone forever.

The goal here is to pay off the debts. For that reason, I don't want you to look at the interest rates on your loans. For most people, it won't make that much difference anyway. So simply pick them off, smallest to largest.

Now, after you pay off the smaller debts, you will have more and more available to pay toward the next debts. Don't change the amount of money you have budgeted for payoffs; instead, as you eliminate each debt, the minimum payment you were paying on that one can now be applied to the next debt down the line. Keep paying on that one until it is gone, then move on to the next one. I can assure you, after you go through this process, you will not be excited about running up your debts again.

Creditor Contact

While you're going through this process, you can contact your creditors to try to get them to lower your interest rate or even stop interest collection completely. You might be surprised how willing to negotiate some creditors can be.

This depends, of course, on who the creditors are. Some are more likely to work with you than others, and your credit history with them will make a difference.

It is best to contact them before you are late on a payment. Don't be afraid to make that phone call. You may be pleasantly surprised at how much less you can spend to get your debts paid off.

And don't be afraid to change credit cards during this process. If you haven't made a late payment and you are transferring your balance, there will always be another credit card company that wants your business.

If you do that, be careful of the fees that many companies are charging to transfer balances. Some cards add a one-time fee of 2 to 3% of the balance to your account. That way, you almost don't notice it, but it is real money and should be treated that way.

Consumer counseling services do much the same thing you are doing yourself with The Debt Eliminator. The good thing those services often can do is get creditors to stop the interest from accumulating while you are paying.

You make one payment each month to these services, and they pay out what you send them. They'll usually charge you around 15% of the debt (which can be less than the interest you were paying). There can also be a list of additional fees hidden in their fine print. And these companies pay your bills in a manner and on a schedule that suits them.

If they don't make your payments on time, or make too small a payment to cover your monthly minimum, your credit will suffer. There have even been complaints that some companies took customers' money and made no payments at all. Be sure you contact your state's Attorney General for information on any credit counseling company you are considering.

If you set up your own plan and make the calls to creditors yourself, I am confident you will accomplish this without a credit counseling company. If you do it on your own, you will spend less money and complete it more quickly, and your credit will heal much faster.

The Bankruptcy Tool

While you are working with a credit counseling company, your credit report will show that you are in a repayment plan, which many lenders look at like a bankruptcy. This method will have negative effects on your credit even after all your debts have been paid off, but, of course, you do get a local counselor to help you.

And, though banks and credit card companies and the federal government have made it tougher, you still can file for bankruptcy.

Bankruptcy is designed as a "do over" for financial miscalculations. Most people think filing for bankruptcy means they are total failures. But bankruptcy is a tool. It is nothing personal. You would be surprised how many people you know have filed for bankruptcy and are now doing very well with their finances.

Bankruptcy allows you to wipe out your debt. You can just walk away from your credit cards, though there are some limits as to what other debts can be included. For example, if you owe money to the government, you will not be able to include it all in your bankruptcy filing.

I am not an attorney, and you will need to contact one to get the exact legal advice you need, about how the law relates to your specific situation and debts.

In my mortgage practice, I have seen the aftermath of bankruptcies as I dealt with clients trying to get a home loan. From a mortgage lender's perspective, here is what I would suggest to make getting a mortgage loan easier after a bankruptcy:

- Make sure every debt you have is included in the bankruptcy. Your attorney should run a credit report from all three credit bureaus, and address every single credit item in the bankruptcy. If anything is missed, you'll have to pay it later. It can't be fixed.
- Every account should have a full and complete account number along with the correct address of each creditor.
- If you keep a debt and continue to make the payments, some of those debts may still appear on your credit report as an unpaid collection for as long as it takes you to pay it off completely. Only when you have paid it off will it stop negatively affecting your credit. This could take years after your bankruptcy, and will make your financial recovery much slower. Make sure your attorney clearly explains each item in your bankruptcy, and how it will affect you later.
- You should immediately send a copy of your discharged bankruptcy paperwork to each of the three credit bureaus, asking them to correct their information on you. They should show each of the accounts as *"included in the bankruptcy,"* with a balance owing of *"zero."*

Bankruptcy is a legitimate avenue for dumping your debt. However, you will notice that it is last on my list, and you will find the negative effects linger for a longer period of time than from other methods. A bankruptcy will stay on your credit report for ten years, though, in most cases, it becomes a non-issue when getting credit after about four years.

As I said earlier, attorneys make money if you file for bankruptcy. Unless they charge you a consultation fee, they won't make any money at all if you don't file. If you are going to an attorney to ask for guidance on this issue, keep this fact in mind.

In a perfect world, whether or not they made money would not change their advice to you; you would get unbiased counseling without regard for the legal fees involved. But we don't live in a perfect world, and I have seen this enter into an attorney's advice many times.

Don't Look Back

Whatever way you choose to dump your debt, be sure to keep focused on the ultimate goal of eliminating it all and living on less than you bring in. Choose one or a combination of the options described, and then stick with your plan. Don't look back. Don't second-guess yourself.

And once you reach the point where your debt is gone and your float account is growing, you will begin, in a very short time, to make even larger strides toward your financial destination.

CHAPTER 11

Your Credit Score

Who's Keeping Score?

Credit reports and credit scores are the gauges lenders use to determine whether you are a good risk for a loan. Lending and interest rate decisions are based on the information found in your credit report.

But where do these reports and scores come from? There are actually three credit bureaus keeping independent files on your finances — TransUnion, Equifax, and Experian. They gather your information and make it available (at a price) to companies that have your permission to see your credit report.

These credit reporting bureaus provide a valuable service to the people and companies who lend money. Lenders need a reliable and consistent source of information on people who want to borrow from them. Other organizations, like insurance companies and even employers, also make decisions about having business relationships with you based on the information in your credit report.

Your credit report contains your whole financial history in one not-so-easy-to-read format. Who you are, where you live, where you work and for how long, are some of the items included.

Every month, each company from which you borrow money sends a report to each of the three credit bureaus telling how much you owe, how much you paid, how much more you borrowed, if you paid on time, how long you've had the account, etc. Each credit bureau adds this new information (usually accurate, though mistakes do happen) to the file it already has on you.

Credit reports include two other very informative sections. One collects data from public records all over the country, including basic reports on tax liens, judgments, and bankruptcies.

But lenders pay particular attention to the other section, which shows the number of inquiries for your report. This tells a prospective lender who else has checked your credit lately. If several companies have, it could be an indicator that you are having problems borrowing money. Or it could show you're in the process of borrowing money from several others at the same time.

What Are They Looking For?

When a lender is considering making you a loan, they will run a credit report. Once they have your permission, it takes only a few seconds to get this information via computer. Depending on what you are borrowing the money for and how much you are borrowing, the lender may want to see your credit report from any or all of the three bureaus. For example, most car dealers use only one, but, if you are buying real estate, lenders want a report showing information from all three.

These reports tell lenders your borrowing history. Most lending decisions are made on the belief that what you've done in the past is a pretty good indication of what you'll do in the future.

So lenders are very interested in finding out if you have made your previous payments on time. If you were late, was it an isolated case or a regular occurrence? Late payments won't even show on your credit report until they are a full thirty days past due. So, if your payment is due on the 5th, and the lender actually receives it on the 20th, your credit report will show it as an on-time payment.

In other words, you have to be really late before it will show up on your credit report, and that's why lenders don't like to see late payments. If they do find late payments on your report, most lenders will charge you extra because your history is saying the loan could be riskier. And your credit report will show those blemishes for seven years.

Lenders also use the report to see how much debt you already have. If they make this loan to you, will you be able to repay the debt or will you be struggling to make the payments? If a lender thinks you may struggle, they may still make you the loan. They'll just charge you a higher interest rate—which will make it even harder to make the payments. Doesn't make sense, does it? I'm just telling you how the system works. I'm not defending it.

Knowing Your Score

About ten years ago, each of the credit companies came out with a credit scoring system designed to help lenders make decisions without having to wade through the pages of information in a standard report. Each bureau has its own procedure that works a little differently, but the actual credit scores they produce turn out to be very close.

The credit scoring system attempts to reduce to a single number your ability and willingness to repay a loan. Your overall credit situation and history are given numerical values and run through a very complicated mathematical formula to arrive at your score. Depending on that score, a lender, insurance company, or employer will draw conclusions about your financial situation, financial practices, and even your organizational skills.

Even though the credit bureaus keep their formulas a secret, I can still give you an idea of how this system works. The most important thing to understand is that it is negatively based. What does this mean? It means that the highest score anyone can get is a 900, and that's where everyone starts. But, as soon as they know your name, you lose points. Every time someone checks your credit when you apply for a loan, you lose points. When you actually borrow money, you lose points. If you charge something on a credit card . . . . You get it.

Going over your credit limit, making late payments (remember, they have to be thirty days late to count), or having lots of debt, collections, judgments, and bankruptcies—they all count against your score.

The deductions from your scores differ based on the frequency and severity of your missteps. More recent lapses weigh more heavily than those that happened months or years ago.

Think of your credit as a wound. If you damage your body, it takes time to heal, and, if you injure yourself again in the same place before it heals completely, the healing process has to start all over again. Credit scores work in much the same way.

Another major factor in lowering your credit scores is the kind of debt you have, and guess which kind lowers your score the most. Yep, consumer debt. This is another part of the reason you need to dump that debt. These systems are set up to reward people who are good with their money. That means you can owe millions of dollars in mortgage debt, and still end up with a much higher credit score than someone who owes $30,000 on credit cards.

Looking at the Numbers

I have seen thousands of credit reports and done a lot of research on top of that. Let me tell you how credit scores break out.

If you are working with a lender that uses a report giving them all three scores, they will throw out the high and the low and use the middle one. If they run two scores, they will use the lower of the two.

The highest credit score I have ever seen was an 828. This person had a long credit history and yet had very little debt. And they had never made a late payment on anything. With a credit score that high, you would be able to borrow money any time, for any reason, at the best rates available.

The lowest score I have ever seen was in the high 400s. The exact number doesn't really matter because, once you get below 540 or so, it will be almost impossible for you to borrow money anyway. If you want to buy a house, you need a minimum of 580.

If you have a score in the range of 580, you probably will be able buy a house, though you may need some down payment money and you'll pay the highest rates available. Don't pay any attention to mortgage advertising because you won't be able to get those rates or terms until your credit heals. So, even though you might be able to get a loan, it may not make sense financially.

Most people have credit scores in the upper 600s. The last report I saw said the average score was about 680. This would qualify you to buy most anything, but, again, it probably won't qualify you for the best interest rates available. Don't expect to get the latest 0% interest car loan unless you have very good credit—most of the time, a score over 700. And, when lenders set a credit score limit for a particular interest rate or credit offer, most companies won't make an exception for even one point off that score.

Ideally, you want to get your score above 740. If you're in that area, you're in the top 10% or so of credit scores in the country. You'll be able to borrow money at the best rates and terms available. In fact, if you are buying something that is good collateral, like a car or a house, high credit scores can eliminate your need to provide verification of your income and maybe even of your job. Lenders already know the best borrowers would rather cut off a finger than make a late payment, so they use a high credit score to predict that their investment will be safe.

Checking and Fixing Your Score

So, how do you check your credit, and what do you do if it needs some help and healing?

Many places will show you your credit report. If you want to pay for it, you can go online or even contact your mortgage lender, which may be easier because you can get all three reports at the same time. If you want a free report, each credit bureau is required by law to provide you one every year at no charge, but you have to request it. (At the end of this chapter you will find contact information for all three bureaus.)

Online, you will find lots of places that will run your credit report for you. Many charge a fee, but their real goal is to get you to pay a fee on a monthly basis, in exchange for their monitoring your credit report for you. They are working on your fear to get you to do this.

If you request a credit report from each bureau once a year, and monitor it for accuracy, you should have no problems. Remember, the goal is to have no consumer debt. So any debt that anyone tries to put on your credit will send up a big red flag.

What do you do if you have had some credit problems in the past and want to fix them? First, I want to tell you that you must be persistent. You will have to write letters to each bureau and continue to follow up until you can verify that the information on your report is now correct.

Don't try to get them to remove information that *is* correct; chances are that won't work. If you owe the debt, plan to pay it. The exception, of course, is if you are filing for bankruptcy.

Start by getting a copy of your credit report and see what's on it. As I said, most people have reasonable credit, so your credit report is probably okay and will be an accurate reflection of your credit history. For most people, there isn't much to fix.

If there are mistakes on your report, you have to contact the bureau that shows the mistake. In your letter, list the exact account, the account number, and specifically tell them what you think the report should say. The bureau has thirty days from the time it receives your request, to prove that they have the correct information, or they have to remove it from your report. They'll contact the actual creditor and verify the information on the report. Most often, the items you will question will be a late payment, or a collection or judgment that has already been paid off.

You don't need to contact the bureaus just because you think the balance on one of your accounts looks a little high. The balances on these reports are at least a month behind.

When you write your letters, be sure to keep copies of everything you send them. That way, if you need to contact them again later, you can send an actual copy. It will be your job to make sure the correct information ends up on your credit report. You will have to do the follow-up.

If your credit reports show you have collection accounts outstanding, you will need to contact the collection agencies. Usually with a phone call you can find out what the debt is for, how much they claim you owe them, and how much they will actually accept to clear the debt off your credit report.

Here are some tips for dealing with collection agencies. First, understand that the people employed by these agencies work on commission. They get a commission on every dollar they collect from you, whether you owe it or not. If you are not sure you owe the debt, make them verify in writing how much you owe and to whom.

They'll immediately want to know who you are and how they can reach you in the future. Most collections are held up because the collectors haven't known how to reach you. They will ask for as much information as you will give them.

The representatives of the collection agency will require you to call them Mr. or Mrs. This is a manipulative ploy to put you down. Keep in mind that whatever name they give you will be a fake. They make up names so angry customers can't find them later. Since they are on commission, most of them have poor to terrible credit, so they've probably been on the other end of a collection phone call, too. Don't let them wreck your day when they start pushing. They are just trying to collect a debt they think you owe. This is their job, and they are good at what they do. They will push.

However, they must be nice to you. They can't call you names or threaten you. They can only call you when you give them permission to do so. If you don't want them calling you at work, tell them not to, and they have to stop. You don't have to give them your work number, but they're good at tracking people down. If you tell them where you work, they will find you. So, don't think that just because you haven't given them your work number, they won't call you at work. They will.

Keep in mind that, if you do owe the debt, the sooner you get it paid off, the sooner you can stop dealing with these people. They don't care about your story. If you owe the money, they only want to hear how and when you are going to pay it back.

When you first call them, they will tell you how much you owe, including interest and penalties. In almost every case, you can settle for the original amount of the debt, and sometimes even less.

If you agree to pay a certain amount on a certain day, do it. Don't make an agreement with them unless you plan to keep it. If you ask them for a deal and you agree to one, you must keep up your end and pay it. If you're not yet ready to pay them off, don't call them. Wait until you're ready because, as soon as they know where you are, they will come after you and try to make some money.

Looking Forward

Cleaning up your credit is a painstaking process, requiring time and persistence.

Don't give up.

Because once you have completed the task, your credit can start to heal. Then you can begin your financial journey all over again, this time looking forward instead of looking back.

Credit Bureau Contact Information

You can try to call, but, in my experience, you only have success in dealing with them by mail or e-mail.

TransUnion PO Box 4000 Chester, PA 19022 866-887-2673	www.transunion.com
Equifax PO Box 740241 Atlanta, GA 30374 800-685-1111	www.equifax.com
Experian PO Box 2002 Allen, TX 75013 888-397-3742	www.experian.com/reportaccess

Conclusion

Now What Do You Do?

I've laid out a considerable amount of information in these pages. Now my concern is that I haven't overwhelmed you.

Most people don't like to think or talk about money. That makes what you have done—reading a book about money and beginning to work on how you handle yours—more than most people are willing to do. That's why most people are living paycheck to paycheck. But you want more than that for yourself and your family, don't you?

If you *are* a little overwhelmed, I've got an easy way for you to get started. Do these three things:

1. Determine where you are in terms of being a saver or a spender. Then make the necessary changes in who has to handle the money. Remember, a saver must handle the money.

2. Set up your spending accounts and redirect your money accordingly.

3. Write down everything you bring in and spend for at least one month.

I promise you: If you do these three things, you will have accomplished more in the one hour it will take than most people do in a lifetime.

Do what you can on these three and if you need or want to, you can contact us at coachme@theeverydaymillionaire.com and let us know what kind of questions or challenges you face for your next step. We'll get back to you with answers for your specific situations.

We'll do that because I believe you will then choose to follow the plan for another month, then another and another. Before you know it, you'll have complete control over your money and be well along the way to your financial destination.

It's a journey you won't take alone. We will continue to provide ongoing support and coaching through our website. Check www.theeverydaymillionaire.com regularly to see the latest tips and materials we're developing to help you achieve your financial vision.

Last Thoughts

I have two final thoughts I want to leave with you.

First, it is important to understand the difference between saving and not spending. If you buy something on sale, you are not saving any money unless you put the difference in prices into your saving account. More than likely you didn't save it, however; you just didn't spend it.

Second, I believe in the bigger pile theory I learned from my business coach. He charges a lot to coach me, but I have learned a great deal, and my money has been well spent.

The bigger pile theory says that you shouldn't trust people with information unless they have a bigger pile than you do. Here's what the bigger pile theory looks like in my life:

- I don't take weight loss advice from people who need to lose weight.
- I don't take childcare advice from people who don't have kids.
- I don't take financial advice from people who don't have more money than I do.

The tragedy I see on a daily basis is people taking financial advice from people who have not applied good financial management in their own lives. If people are struggling with their money, don't trust them with yours. If people aren't achieving prosperity in their own lives, they have not earned the right to offer advice in yours.

So, if you are considering working with someone to help with your finances, ask them the tough questions.

Before you hire a stockbroker, find out how much is in his or her portfolio, and how that money is invested.

If you are asking an attorney for advice about a bankruptcy, only to find out he is currently in bankruptcy himself, move on.

A real estate agent who doesn't own a house should not be your agent. They should have several years of experience, or they are not qualified to work for you.

Your mortgage is the single largest debt you will have. Only take advice from someone with exceptional credit who owns at least one or two properties. They should be financially stable, or the advice they give you may not be based on your best interest. If they are not financially stable, they may not even know what good advice is.

The bottom line is, you can fix whatever is not working. The right advice for you is out there. There's an old saying that illustrates this very well:

"When the student is ready, the teacher will appear."

You are ready.